REAL AMBITION

Quit dreaming and create success your way

D0062298

PSYCHOLOGIES
MAGAZINE

This edition first published 2016
© 2016 Kelsey Publishing Ltd

Registered office
John Wiley and Sons Ltd, The Atrium, Southern Gate, Chichester, West Sussex, PO19 8SQ,
United Kingdom

For details of our global editorial offices, for customer services and for information about
how to apply for permission to reuse the copyright material in this book please see our
website at www.wiley.com.

Library of Congress Cataloging-in-Publication Data is available

A catalogue record for this book is available from the British Library.

ISBN 978-0-857-08663-1 (pbk)
ISBN 978-0-857-08664-8 (ebk)   ISBN 978-0-857-08665-5 (ebk)

Cover design: Wiley

Set in 9.5/13pt ITC Franklin Gothic Std by Aptara, New Delhi, India

Printed in Great Britain by TJ International Ltd, Padstow, Cornwall, UK

CONTENTS

FOREWORD

by Suzy Greaves, Editor, Psychologies

Our ethos at *Psychologies* magazine is 'your life, your way.' This book is how to live that ethos. Real ambition is about defining success on your own terms. We are all unique and when we tune into what we *really* want versus the world's definition of success, it's the ultimate ticket to freedom. Why? Because then you can start to build a life around your values and what you love instead of wasting your energy comparing and competing for something you never really wanted in the first place.

To discover your real ambition, you *do* need to spend some time working on your life versus being in it. This book invites you to dig deep and work out what really does inspire and fulfil you. It's a space to press pause while you complete the exercises and quizzes to discover what is your real ambition and then to create a new life plan from there – be it changing career, learning how to create your own business or writing a novel.

Real Ambition will help you get clear about goals that make sense to you. But it's not just about doing, but being. It's an invitation to make a leap to be your best self, to create a life that inspires you versus just making do, to have the courage to learn something new, to risk failing so you can create a life that reflects your real values.

When you have real ambition, life feels easier because you are comfortable in your own skin and living life authentically. You inspire, you lead and excel because you are living a successful life – defined by you.

Are you ready? Let's make it happen.

Suzy Greaves, Editor, *Psychologies*

INTRODUCTION

We're so pleased you decided to buy this book about Real Ambition because at *Psychologies* magazine we believe that the link between ambition and success is the word *real*. And by real we mean what feels good for you. We want to kick off by telling you that your interest in *real* ambition indicates that your mind is tuned to the right wavelength for determining your success.

At this point we know that you have established a need to find out how to achieve success. Perhaps you sense that you need to learn more about how ambition works and what steps you can take to harness your own ambition. You may have one particular ambition in your life, but maybe something makes you feel unsure about whether it's possible to achieve this. Or maybe ambition for you isn't based on a singular mission and instead is about figuring out how to be successful. Or you might be at a dead end and want to know how to get out of this and what else might be possible. You may even be doing perfectly OK, but don't want to live an OK life — you want to know if and how it's feasible to achieve an amazing life.

So there are all sorts of reasons why you might have bought this book. At *Psychologies* magazine we know that the one thing our readers have in common is that they are striving for better lives all round. A better life for our readers isn't just about external and conventional marks of success. A better life is as much about inner wellbeing. We know from the therapists and life coaches who write for us, as well as those we interview every month for the magazine, that success is a huge preoccupation for their clients. People get caught up in feeling they haven't achieved 'enough', or they beat themselves up because they feel they are inadequate.

How to be successful has been a big question since the eighties. There are countless books about this. So what makes *Real Ambition* any different? We have for some time sensed both from the experts we have access to, the academic research we follow, and the feedback from our readers, that there is a major cultural shift in what constitutes success. We've had the 'yuppies' (young upwardly mobile) of the eighties, the high-flyers of the nineties, and the mass consumerism of the noughties. In more recent years, success in our culture has come to be associated with how high-flying city figures and reality TV stars behave. But now that we're slowly exiting a recession in the UK, we believe that there's a strong sense of wanting to rewrite the meaning of ambition and success.

Real Ambition aims to help you create your own meaning of success and to encourage you to create a model of ambition that suits you. This involves first understanding who you are at this point.

We believe that ambition is that desire to make the inner leap to *be* your best self so that you can live your best life. Instead of 'making do', it's all about the doing. And of course that comes down to courage. Our job is to help you find that courage, show you how to harness and maximize it so that you don't turn back, or give up. Right now it's like you're looking at a map, your eyes are on your destination, and you're questioning the transport. We want to encourage you to look further than your destination, to create a journey to that point that enriches your life from day one, a journey that's fascinating and opens up your mind constantly.

If you have formed the belief that ambition is about being a certain personality type, and you think this book will be about becoming that personality – well, we don't believe this is the case. Ambition is not about those people you read about, or certain people you know. We won't be advocating that you must fake being anything you're not.

Healthy ambition and a successful life are based on feeling fulfilled: it's about what makes you want to get-up-and-go every day, what makes you feel the best you. It's about knowing what really nourishes your life. And that might very well be different to what nourishes (and inspires) all your friends, your colleagues, your family and everyone else around you.

The foundation of healthy ambition is the belief that you deserve the best life for you, and then creating a plan to make it happen. It's about knowing how to be equipped so that you can follow the plan or, if necessary, change the plan to a better one. The plan won't be in your head. Think in terms of planning an adventure that you fully intend to enjoy.

HOW TO USE THIS BOOK

We've divided this book into three parts:

1. What Does Ambition Mean to You?
2. What's Stopping You from Achieving Your Ambitions?
3. How Can You Achieve Your Ambitions?

In Part 1 you'll gain an overview of ambition and success in our culture, how this is changing, and what this means to you. You may discover that you're more successful than you think. You'll be inspired to create your own model of success rather than accepting what's given to you by the media, celebrity culture or people around you.

In Part 2 we'll help you understand why you feel you're not achieving your dreams and how to turn things around. In Part 3 we show you how to engage your mind to go from goals to action and give you advice that you can apply in every area of your life. We don't want to keep you waiting until the final part to start making things happen though, so throughout the book you'll find tips designed to act as ambition boosters that you can try out immediately to help fuel your dreams.

At the end of Chapters 1–3 and 5 there are tests so that you can assess yourself. We've also included key 'Ask Yourself' questions for you to reflect on, so that you can relate each chapter to your personal experience. You will also find case studies from real people (with names and identifying circumstances changed). We chose these case studies so that you can see how ambition and success differ from person to person.

We carefully selected a panel of five leading experts to interview, each one with a different specialization, perspective and background. Two of our experts started their professional lives as actors, two have business backgrounds and one is an academic. Choosing a mix of experts is always exciting because although we know the individual experts well, we have no idea how what they say individually on the subject will gel collectively. We set out to give you a mix that will maximize the advice available to you. What turned out to be fascinating for us is that all our experts were on the same page as us: our culture is changing to one based on being individuals, rather than toeing a line fed to us.

We hope you will be inspired to believe that you can create your vision of success, that you will take the actions to make this happen, and that the process will be rewarding.

THE EXPERTS INTERVIEWED FOR *REAL AMBITION*

Kele Baker, mind-body-movement coach

Kele Baker helps people take control of their health and wellbeing by teaching body awareness, coordination, relaxation, self-discovery and self-healthcare through tai chi, qigong, the Alexander Technique and mindfulness.

She is a former co-director of Kensington Dance Studio with over 20 years' experience teaching and choreographing for stage and television. Baker is the author of *Strictly Come Dancing: Step By Step Dance Class* (BBC Books) and director of the Life Force Chi Centre.

http://www.kelebaker.com
http://www.lifeforcechicentre.com

Chris Baréz-Brown, creative and business beatnik

Chris Baréz-Brown and his consultancy Upping Your Elvis show corporate teams how to unleash their creativity for more successful branding and a happy workplace. His background includes helping turn Carling Black Label into a billion-pound brand.

Baréz-Brown is the author of three bestselling books: *How to Have Kick Ass Ideas* (Harper Collins), *Shine. How to Survive and Thrive at Work* (Penguin), *Free! Love Your Work, Love Your Life* (Penguin) and the latest *Wake Up!* (Penguin Life, 2016).

www.uppingyourelvis.com
@BarezBrown

Dannie-Lu Carr, creativity specialist, communications consultant and creative practitioner

Dannie-Lu Carr works with individuals and organizations on creativity and communications. She has worked with a wide range of corporate, media, PR, education and public sector companies, from Bloomberg through to the NHS.

Carr is the author of *Brilliant Assertiveness* (Pearson). She writes and directs for her production company Flaming Poppy, and runs acting workshops. Following a TEDx talk in 2015 she formed Reorientations to campaign for cultural change in the arts.

www.dannielucarr.com
www.flamingpoppy.com
www.reorientations.co.uk
@DannieLu

John Purkiss, headhunter and coach

John Purkiss runs workshops and coaches individuals on personal branding and personal development. He is the co-founder of Purkiss&Company where he recruits chief executives, finance directors and other board members.

Purkiss is the co-author of three books including *Brand You – Turn Your Unique Talents into a Winning Formula* (Pearson) which has been translated into five languages. He is working on a new book which will be called *The Art of Letting Go.*

www.johnpurkiss.com

www.brandyou.info

Lisa Fortlouis Wood, Professor of Psychology and licensed clinical psychologist

Professor Fortlouis Wood teaches clinical psychology (including psychotherapy) at the University of Puget Sound, Tacoma, Washington and also practises as a clinical psychologist. Her specializations include family communication, relationship therapy, community, psychology and social/personal identity.

Professor Fortlouis Wood is regularly invited to present her research findings at educational conferences all over the world. Her most recent research (with Galena K. Rhoades, University of Denver) was on the effect of emotional distress in the family on college students.

www.pugetsound.edu

1 WHAT DOES AMBITION MEAN TO YOU?

CHAPTER 1

REDEFINING AMBITION AND SUCCESS

The meaning of ambition and success is something that varies from person to person. What success means to you or what you want to see for yourself in the future might be completely different to someone else's interpretation. Perhaps you dream of making it in a highly competitive arts and entertainment field like Hollywood, the music charts, the *New York Times* bestseller list. You might want to escape a dreary no-status job for an exciting high-level career. You might be determined to make so much money you don't have to ever worry about it. Or you might have decided to totally change your life by moving to a different city or even another country.

Before we help you learn how to achieve your ambitions and create success in your life, you need to be clear about what ambition and success mean. If your definitions are simply the opposite of terms like unsuccessful, failure, mediocre or boring, you won't be clear about what exactly you are aiming to create. So what do ambition and success mean generally – and what do they mean to you?

ARE DICTIONARY DEFINITIONS RIGHT?

We're starting with dictionary definitions of ambition and success because we want to strip them down from all the associations you may have made about both words. Think of a house that someone has painted over again and again, and that needs to be stripped back to a shell and rebuilt to achieve a home that's redesigned and redecorated properly as well as beautifully. The same has happened to these big concepts of ambition and success. They have become overloaded with the meanings you've absorbed around you. One of the things we're aiming to do is to help you redefine ambition and success on your terms.

So let's get to the basics. According to the *Oxford Dictionary* ambition is:

A strong desire to do or achieve something
Desire and determination to achieve success

On the online Dictionary.com we find ambition described as:

An earnest desire for some type of achievement or distinction, as power, honor, fame, or wealth, and the willingness to strive for its attainment

In the *Oxford Dictionary* there are various definitions of success:

The accomplishment of an aim or purpose
The attainment of fame, wealth, or social status
A person or thing that achieves desired aims or attains fame, wealth

All the above definitions are food for thought aren't they?
It's evident that the classic definitions of ambition are about wanting to accomplish an aim that is connected to success, and that the overall definitions of success are based on accomplishing goals that are invariably connected to wealth and status.

By flagging up these definitions we may have depressed you a teeny bit. There may be a thought at the back of your mind that there are people who have a knack of rising to the top and making money and having everything, but you're not that type. But you don't have to be that or any type.

> **❝A definition of ambition based on seeking and aspiring to *something* gives each of us the opportunity to choose what we want to achieve.❞**

Kele Baker, mind-body-movement coach

Who says we have to accept dictionary definitions? Think of all those modern words that only in recent years have entered dictionaries, like Google, text and smartphone. Who says ambition has to go hand in hand with success, or that success is dependent on a certain type of ambition? If ambition is the desire to achieve a goal and that goal is happiness, or fulfilment, isn't that success? How about if you substitute the word 'wealth' with 'prosperity', and the word 'fame' with 'recognition'? Think about this and it will click: you have an approachable vision of success that relates to *you*.

So let's look at how you can reformulate ambition and success in a way that works for you.

REAL AMBITION ISN'T RUTHLESS

Over the decades, ambition has come to be associated with a type of ruthless, overconfident person who will stop at nothing to achieve what they're after. Ambition is associated with dog-eats-dog environments where people are hard-nosed and heartless, self-obsessed and egocentric.

But why should a desire to make a dream come true mean having to be a caricature of ambition? We're certainly not going to give you the secrets of ruthless successful people that work while leaving out the bad bits, because this book is about developing a holistic approach. When your ambition nurtures you, we believe that the rest follows.

Old-style ambition has simply fallen flat on its face. We know that thanks to one word: recession. The most ambitious people, those who were the most ruthless and the wealthiest, wiped out entire economies. We don't propose to get into a discussion on economics and politics here. But we hope the brief reminder of this period in our history will help to show that you don't need the traits traditionally associated with ambition. Being ruthless, cut-throat and hard won't serve you as a person or your wellbeing, and won't benefit humanity.

66 Ambition is often seen as achieving things at the expense of others. 99

John Purkiss, headhunter and coach

Whether you have a specific dream or you're looking for a way to create a specific life, you may be wondering whether you need a watered-down version of ruthless, some sort of healthy go-go-go. The problem with old-style ambition is that any form of go-go-go can lead to imbalance. Think of workaholics and anyone you know who works relentlessly and doesn't have a life and you'll get the picture.

One of the blocks stopping you might even be a fear that to make your dreams happen you'll have to give up friends and hobbies and isolate yourself. This certainly isn't the kind of success we have in mind.

OLD-STYLE AMBITION IS BURNOUT – REAL AMBITION IS BALANCE

If you believe that success is either down to luck or working at your goals non-stop that's not surprising. This is the society we live in. Our TV is dominated by reality TV stars who've become famous for not really doing anything, the media is full of overnight success stories, yet all around us we see people working hard to find jobs or keep their jobs.

66 We live in a dynamic, forceful, moving, active society. We have to constantly *do* and *achieve*. Yet this is a burnt out and stressed society. 99

Kele Baker, mind-body-movement coach

As somebody now working to help people find inner peace and maintain this peace in their outer lives, mind-body-movement coach Kele Baker is acutely aware of how stressed people are in modern lives. Her long-time interest in Chinese medicine and philosophy helped her deal with her own stress and breakdown as a young actress in New York and she maintained this interest through moving on to different occupations as a ballroom dance teacher, Alexander Technique practitioner, co-director of a dance school business, as a choreographer and working on one of the UK's most popular TV programmes.

Baker believes that our Western lives need ancient wisdom to realign them. 'We need balance, rest and rejuvenation.' It might seem odd to talk about resting in a book about achieving success. After all, shouldn't that come later? Might rest not turn into laziness? Does rest really fit in with ambition?

That's the thing about real ambition: you can evaluate what you want. If there's a way to achieve your dreams without burning out from exhaustion, wouldn't you rather do that?

" Ambition needs balance and it might take a while to get there. "

Dannie-Lu Carr, creativity specialist, communications consultant & creative practitioner

There's no doubt that the pace of our modern lives, especially in cities, is fast and demanding. It's also inevitable that one of your desires, more often than not work, will become all consuming, particularly in a competitive field or an economic climate where jobs aren't easy to find. But if you only feed that strand in your life, what will happen to the other areas? If you had a garden and only looked after the roses and ignored the rest, it wouldn't be a very pretty sight would it?

BOOST YOUR BRAIN

Recent research by the National Institute of Mental Health[1] in the USA showed that the more successful people are, the more key parts of the brain tend to 'talk' with each other during a resting state. In other words, success and satisfaction with life boosts the brain and makes it stronger.

You can start thinking success and boosting your brain right now. Can you learn something new? Can you improve your finances by striking new deals for your utilities? Can you give yourself a new mental challenge like learning some basics in a new language so you can speak when you're on holiday? Can you make a simple lifestyle change that will make your days even marginally better?

As a coach working both in business and the arts, Dannie-Lu Carr observes people exhausting themselves hoping this will lead to what they want. Yet she's adamant that 'over-focusing' is counterproductive and working to the point of exhaustion is *not* what gets you from ambition to success. 'It could take time to achieve your main dream, so you need balance in your life in order to keep going and not give up. Things have to be in balance: love, self-respect, leisure, self-nurturing, friends.'

Anyone who has made the transition from unhealthy to healthy probably recognizes that balance is far from easy. Getting into the habit of shopping for fresh food, learning to make wholesome food, finding a fitness routine that doesn't feel like a regime, resisting anything digital before sleeping – none of this is easy when it's new. On a larger scale, a balanced life requires thinking, planning, trying, doing. The process can feel a little sticky to begin with, but then this is what you will want to embrace all the time.

By addressing all areas in your life, what you are effectively building is a sound foundation that will boost the bit that might be toughest to achieve. In other words, you are creating an inner support system that nurtures you.

Are we really saying that ambition can be nurturing?

REAL AMBITION IS NURTURING

Old-style ambition doesn't nurture us as individuals, nor does it nurture a healthy work environment, community or the world at large. *Real* ambition, however, can not only sustain our dreams, it can sustain our wellbeing *and* the wellbeing of others.

Before you wonder whether we're getting all abstract and New-Agey, bear with us a little. Have you ever done any of the following?

* Made an effort to recycle
* Sponsored someone who was raising money for a cause
* Taken care of a sick relative or friend
* Donated goods to a charity
* Taught somebody something you know

- Made somebody a birthday cake
- Treated a friend to a night out.

What we're getting at is that it's likely that you're already doing something nurturing. You're already not selfish. As Baker puts it, we're aware that we're 'over-taking from ourselves and the environment'. We know we have to put something back in to ourselves as individuals – and to the planet as a whole.

> **66 Ambition is having drive and enthusiasm towards a clear goal for a positive purpose. 99**
>
> Dannie-Lu Carr, creativity specialist, communications consultant & creative practitioner

We live in very difficult times politically and economically. We watch the news and more often than not it's gruesome. But we also live in very exciting times of change. Carr points to the new wave of 'social-preneurs' like former jewellery business couple John and Cynthia Hardy who set up the eco-friendly and holistic Green School[2] in Bali, Indonesia: 'Social preneurs are creating new paradigms for success in business on an individual level and community level, so it's a win-win for everyone.'

One of the reasons we felt it was the right to time to write about ambition is because of these new paradigms that are emerging. Ambition might not be new, but it's not static. It's ever-changing.

AMBITION IS HUMAN – AND HUMANS EVOLVE

We know from anthropology that wherever there are communities of human beings, there will always be humans who want more. In a *Time Magazine* cover story on ambition in 2005,[3] anthropologist Edward Lowe at Soka University of America was quoted as saying that 'Ambition is an evolutionary product'. What's more it has always differed. 'No matter how social status is defined, there are certain people in every community who aggressively pursue it and others who aren't so aggressive.' Lowe spelt out for the magazine that people want more than the basics. 'It's fundamentally human to be prestige conscious,' he said.

In an article we published in 2012,[4] 'Is ambition a dirty word?', our big question was whether conflicted attitudes were holding women back. What our journalist Anita Chaudhuri found through her research was that both men and women want to achieve recognition. However, whereas men don't have a problem owning up to being ambitious and thrive on competitiveness, women shy away from being seen as ego-driven. Men tend to focus on one ambition, while women have more of a variety of goals.

A central question in this article was why there were fewer women at boardroom level. Fewer women seemed driven to succeed in male-dominated worlds like finance; instead they seemed drawn to more 'caring' or 'female' areas like charities or fashion. Yet the piece concluded by pointing to a change in attitudes as a result of the recession, with a younger female generation feeling more comfortable about ambition and older generations of men realizing that old-style ambition comes at a price

> **"Success for me now is about hanging out with my kids (aged 8 and 10) when they come home from school. I know that when I'm stressed I don't switch off and so I don't engage with them."**

Chris Baréz-Brown, creative and business beatnik

In just four years since we ran this piece, we believe the meaning of ambition has shifted and changed even more for both men and women. Both genders are seeking ambition that is acceptable, natural and positive.

PROFESSOR FORTLOUIS WOOD'S DEFINITION OF REAL AMBITION

- *'Having the creative drive to go beyond what is currently visible or available*
- *Seeing something new rather than playing it safe*
- *Finding new goals, and then striving to realize them*
- *Striving to create something new, and taking risks to do so*
- *Wanting to learn and wanting to grow; it's tenacity plus drive.*

Ambition is:

> *I have an idea that is worth pursuing and it matters to me.*
> *I want to see how my idea turns out – even if it needs revision or is wrong.*
> *How will my idea work and what can I learn by testing it?*
> *What can I do with my new idea? What will my new idea do?'*

If you were curious about ambition and success we hope we've sparked in you a desire to formulate your own definitions for your own unique visions. You don't have to become that stereotypical, outdated ambitious person who could risk becoming unlikeable or unhealthy or unhappy, or all three.

Although you might have one overriding dream, you don't have to limit yourself. It's healthier to think about all areas of one's life because a balanced life is a healthy, fulfilled life.

Real success is living a life that is based on your values and your values alone, not what everybody else wants. You may have grown up with your family influencing your view of success, but remember that was based on their circumstances. Your friends might be following a similar path, whether it's working in a particular sector or getting married, but that's not a reason to do the same. You might get the impression from social media and the media at large that success is about wanting certain things, but you don't have to choose them too. You can choose something else.

Remember, it's your life, your way. That means there's no need to compare and compete. When you're true to being you, you won't need to. Once you click into what you really desire, you'll be excited about getting there, and that will make you a happier person to be with – so you'll attract new people, new opportunities and, of course, success.

66 My ambition is to live each day well. If I achieve that, I am a very happy boy. 99

Chris Baréz-Brown, creative and business beatnik

ASK YOURSELF

Q What do you associate ambition with?

Q Who do you associate ambition with – what sort of person is this? What do you have in common with this person?

Q What did ambition mean to you when you bought this book? What does it mean to you now?

Q Do you have one central ambition? What is it?

Q Can you begin to formulate what you desire in different areas of your life?

Q What does achieving success mean to you?

Q If you could rewrite the definitions of ambition and success to suit you, how would these definitions reflect who you are?

HOW DO YOU DEFINE SUCCESS?
Find out what really matters to you now

Sometimes we can lose sight of what really matters to us, especially when we're on the receiving end of other people's ideas of success, whether from the media (40,000 followers on Instagram anyone?) or our parents (a steady job, a nice house and savings in the bank sound familiar?). Then there's our peers – when a friend announces they've been promoted to the next rung on the corporate ladder, are setting up their own business or giving up their job to volunteer abroad, it's hard not to think 'should I be doing that too?' But identifying and shaping your *own* definition of success is like having a Sat Nav for your ambition – instead of setting off and hoping you're going in the right direction, you can steadily journey towards your destination.

The following test will help you get in touch with your genuine ambitions by working out what success means to you. With this and the other quizzes in this book, you'll get the most out of it by selecting the answer that reflects how you usually feel or react, rather than ticking what you think is the 'right' answer (there is no right answer!). Some questions may be about situations that don't apply to you. In that case, take time to consider how you would feel or react in that situation, and select the answer which reflects that most closely.

Test by Sally Brown

QUESTION 1

A magic genie appears and offers you four options. Which would you choose?

A. CEO of an innovative start-up that makes a significant difference to the lives of vulnerable people in your community.

B. A promotion that comes with prestigious job title reflecting your skills and achievements.

C. A part-time job you enjoy but that makes you enough money to live comfortably.

D. A big break in a creative field such as writing or performing.

QUESTION 2

You're asked to represent your company at an international conference in LA. How do you react?

A. You jump at the chance. It's an opportunity to raise your profile both inside and outside your company.

B. You wonder if there'll be time to do a creative retreat or workshop while you're out there.

C. You scan the agenda to see if there will be any speakers talking about social change.

D. You're pleased to be asked but worry about the time away from home.

QUESTION 3

Whose autobiography are you most likely to read?

A. Someone who's rethinking the work-life balance, like Tim Ferriss or Ariana Huffington.

B. A human rights campaigner like Malala Yousafzai or Nelson Mandela.

C. A film director like Steven Spielberg or novelist like JK Rowling.

D. A high-profile business success like Mark Zuckerberg or Sheryl Sandberg.

QUESTION 4

What worry is most likely to keep you up at night?

A. Not spending enough quality time with your family.

B. A colleague at work being promoted above you.

C. A shocking story of injustice or poverty that you've watched on the news.

D. Getting a really bad review of a performance or piece of work.

QUESTION 5

Which of these descriptions would you be most pleased to see in your obituary?

A. 'Widely recognized for his/her achievements in the field.'

B. 'A tireless social campaigner.'

C. 'A wise and calm presence who had time for all.'

D. 'A gifted performer/writer/artist.'

QUESTION 6

Imagine you won enough money so that you no longer had to work. Would you give up your job?

A. In a heartbeat! I'd love the opportunity to simply slow down and savour life.

B. Yes, but I would set up my own charity or campaigning group instead.

C. Yes, so I could finally focus on developing my writing/creating/performing/baking skills.

D. Not necessarily. I couldn't imagine never working again.

QUESTION 7

When was the last time you experienced 'flow' (you were so immersed in what you were doing that you lost track of time)?

A. Spending time on my latest creative project.

B. Going for a walk with a loved one (be it friend, family or four-legged).

C. Brainstorming a fundraising idea.

D. Preparing for an important meeting when it was crucial to make a good impression.

QUESTION 8

When you feel an instant connection with someone, which of these qualities are they most likely to possess?

A. Kindness and compassion.
B. Determination.
C. A creative drive.
D. Calmness and self-assurance.

Now, add up your scores from each answer using the following table, and find out how you define success:

	A	B	C	D
Q1	3	1	2	4
Q2	1	4	3	2
Q3	2	3	4	1
Q4	2	1	3	4
Q5	1	3	2	4
Q6	2	3	4	1
Q7	4	2	3	1
Q8	3	1	4	2

If you scored between 8 and 13 ...

Success for you is about fulfilling your potential

You're willing to take risks and you're good at thinking big picture. You love new ideas and feel sure you have the motivation and focus to make a business or big job a success, if only you knew where you should apply your efforts.

You have an innate competitive drive that works both for and against you. It gives you the drive to keep going, but the desire to 'win' can also send you off in the wrong direction – ever wondered why victory feels hollow? Other people may already consider you successful, and express bemusement at why you seem to want more. But you have a drive to learn and grow and become your best possible self, and that means never resting on your laurels.

Your weakness is that at times there are so many ideas buzzing around your head, you don't give any of them the focus they need to get them off the ground. Working through the chapters in this book should help you crystallize your current priorities.

If you scored between 14 and 20 ...

Success for you is about great quality of life

You're conscientious and motivated, but can find it hard to say no, which takes its toll on your quality of life. You may have experienced issues with ongoing health niggles, energy levels or low mood, and come to the realization that for you, a happy life is all about balance. You know that success is about having enough money to remove financial stress, not racking up thousands in the bank. You're no longer happy just to 'get through' your working days, or live for the weekends and holidays. Sometimes, it's the death of someone close to us that brings home the 'life is short' message. Or it may be that a life-change, like becoming a parent, has made you re-evaluate what really matters to you. Working through this book will help you clarify the changes you need to make to achieve this balance.

If you scored between 21 and 27 …

Success for you is about making a difference

For you, personal success only counts if there's a knock-on benefit for other people, whether it's your local community or the wider world. You may well have already achieved considerable personal success and been left wondering, 'Is this it?' The idea of becoming a social-preneur is very appealing, and you feel especially inspired by those who have tapped into new and innovative ways of working that help other people. You feel acutely aware of issues such as climate change, poverty and social injustice, and are no stranger to charity or voluntary work. But you may have now reached a point where you want to do more, and you're ready to shape your working life accordingly. Read on to learn how to channel this passion in the most effective way.

If you scored between 28 and 32 …

Success for you is about being creative

Ideas and innovation are important to you, and you're searching for a way of developing your passion for creating, either in your working or personal life. Creative types are blessed with an active imagination, but the flipside is that this often comes with anxiety, and you may worry about the future and whether you're 'good enough' to make a career from your creative talents. But as you may well have already discovered, success can feel hollow if it's not an achievement we feel proud of. The good news is that you can bring creativity to most jobs and careers, as well as nurturing this side of you in your personal life. Creativity is a gift that will always be with you – read on to find out how to maximize this positive force in your life to support your ambition.

CHAPTER 2

WHAT DO YOU REALLY WANT?

I magine you're going into a new restaurant. You know the dishes you love and these are the ones you always eat and enjoy. There are others you'd like to try but they might be too expensive, or you don't want to make a fool of yourself with something like lobster or oysters because you're not quite sure how you're meant to eat them. Finally there might be dishes you've never even considered before because you've never seen them on a menu.

It's very easy to go through life doing the same things every day without even realizing you're doing so until something happens that brings change. Going to the same restaurant and eating the same dishes is familiar, safe and there's a sense of stability and security that comes from wonderful memories. But sometimes our favourite, familiar places change or, for whatever reason, we need a change.

> **❝Ambitious people aren't very good at doing the same thing for very long. It's not negative boredom but a craving for newness, energy, fun.❞**
>
> Chris Baréz-Brown, creative and business beatnik

It's the same when thinking about what your ambitions are and what you really want in life. You may know what you want for sure, or you might think you know what you want, or you might have never thought about it. We're not going to ask you to put yourself into one of these categories because at this stage you'll probably discover that your desires fall into all three of them. When we think of success in a balanced way, there will be different ambitions, each at a different stage. This is perfectly normal. It is in fact a healthy and essential part of deciding what you want.

At the same time, figuring out *why* we want something is far trickier than deciding *what* we want. Yet this is the key to success. Success is about creating a full and fulfilled life. To do this you need to find out what you truly want and need in all areas of your life. This means that the more you know yourself, the easier it is to figure out what you need. The more work you do on understanding yourself and what makes you *you*, then the more information you can gather on what you need for your journey and destination. That way you will be excited rather than panicky, well-equipped rather than missing essentials, prepared for obstacles rather than having to give up, and open to different possibilities along the way rather than feeling thrown when something comes up.

Of course, you might already be very clear about something you want, but don't be tempted to skip this chapter. Foremost in your mind there might be a desire to be a super entrepreneur, film star, fashion designer, pop star or politician. Conversely you might have a strong feeling that you want to make lots of money and have a certain lifestyle – but you're frustrated because you don't know how and that's the bit you want to get to. Whichever end of the scale you're at, and everything in between, unravelling what and why lays the foundations of how.

66 Want can come from fear, such as the fear of having no money, or the fear of being alone. 99

John Purkiss, headhunter and coach

IS IT MONEY YOU WANT – OR SOMETHING ELSE?

It's inevitable that one of the most popular wants is money. If you think we're going to sway you away from that, we're not. We live in the real world. For those who can't get on the job ladder or have lost their job, for couples who can't afford to have a family, for hardworking professionals who can't afford their own property and are trapped in high rents, we know that dismissing money concerns isn't an option. So instead of talking about money being meaningless, we're instead going to encourage you to think about money in more depth.

What's important is that you are clear about needing financial stability. Perhaps that might be the first step to creating a sound foundation so that you can then pursue your dreams. What we're getting at is that money itself might not be the dream.

In our society, money and materialism are still very much associated with success. We recycle fanatically, our political leaders discuss climate control, yet come Black Friday and the Christmas sales it's all about shopping. It's not easy to escape material desires – we all want to look great, we all want to live in gorgeous surroundings. Striking a balance between creating a beautiful environment for ourselves and presenting ourselves to reflect our inner personalities – without becoming driven by materialism – isn't easy. We need to work at it.

66 Get away from ambition that is only about money. 99

Chris Baréz-Brown, creative and business beatnik

As our creative and business beatnik expert Chris Baréz-Brown puts it, we need our North Star to guide us, we need a quality vision. During financially challenging times in particular it can be easy to fall into the trap of focusing on money alone. You may think you want lots of money because it would make you happy and solve all your financial worries. There's a huge difference though between having enough so as not to worry – and having much more. Research[1] in 2015 has shown that being wealthy can in fact reduce people's ability to enjoy simple experiences, whereas money spent on *doing* creates more positive feelings than money spent on material items.

Recent research[2] from the University of California, Berkeley, pointed to respect rather than money being more important to overall happiness. The study examined how people felt in relation to their status and found correlations between their happiness levels and changes in their status. So, for example, if you are experiencing depression and money worries having lost your job, winning the lottery would certainly pay off debts and stop you worrying about money. However, if your lost job gave you a feeling that you mattered, then winning the lottery won't help you feel truly happy inside.

One of the biggest studies on money across 63 countries found that freedom and personal autonomy matter far more than money. The in-depth study[3] (consisting of three related studies and four sets of data) by researchers at the Victoria University of Wellington in New Zealand discovered that when people feel more in control of their lives, regardless of how wealthy they are, they feel better. Though money certainly adds to feeling independent, the researchers found it doesn't add to happiness. So if you've found a good job and you find that you can afford nice clothes and holidays, but you're still living at home because you're saving up for your own property, the immediate enjoyment of spending money is cancelled out by the frustration of being an adult living with your parents and not being able to have your own home that you can decorate the way you want, and where you can do what you want. A woman married to a man who is in the top 10 per cent of earners in the country, but who has to toe her husband's line because he makes the money, won't be happy.

Certainly there is a link between increasing your income and life satisfaction. A study[4] by mathematical economists Professor Christian Bayer from the University of Bonn and Professor Falko Jüssen from Bergische Universität Wuppertal looked at how earning and working longer hours affected life satisfaction. They found that more money does make people happier – if the increase is long term. They also found consistently working long hours depletes happiness levels. Their conclusion was that an increase in satisfaction from life comes from working the same hours for more money.

> **" Do you need money to create something amazing that you really want to do? Or do you want to do something in order to make money? "**
>
> Dannie-Lu Carr, creativity specialist, communications consultant & creative practitioner

MEN, WOMEN AND WANTS

There is a view that ambition is male, and that women who are ambitious are like men, but we're not going to subscribe to this because it's an old, unhealthy view of ambition. As we saw in Chapter 1, women previously shied away from expressing their outward ambitions, but things are changing because the concept of ambition is changing. We're over the hangover of the ruthless definition, male or female. Real ambition is about choosing what we want as individuals. That doesn't mean, however, that we ignore gender differences. An understanding of what other men and women around you want and the extent to which you are influenced is important for you to formulate your own ideas.

A four-decade study[5] on a mathematically gifted group found that the group made extraordinary accomplishments by midlife, and had high levels of life satisfaction. One of the most interesting aspects of the research was the discovery that men and women pursued and defined career, family and success in different ways. The main difference was in how men and women allocated their time. Only 65% of women worked full time compared to 90% of men. Men chose careers that required over 50 hours work a week, whereas women defined their success to include time for family and community. All of the men, that's 100%, were willing to devote more than 40 hours a week to their ideal job, compared to 70% of women. When it came to values, for men this was full-time work and a high income, for women it was part-time work, community, family, close relationships and community service.

Yet both men and women agreed that by far the most important element for a meaningful life is family. What differed was how they chose to invest in family: for the men it was making a contribution that could be measured, for women it was about investing time.

Since this study there have been seismic cultural changes. More and more men, including Baréz-Brown, are tearing up the male script of going off to work long hours, and are working from home so that they can spend more time with their children. At the heart of the above study is the notion of what's meaningful for both genders. And it's the same. The study is fascinating because of the detailed questions it asked and the different areas of life it addressed. The people featured in this extensive study over several years were extraordinarily gifted and therefore able to gain very well-paid jobs. Yet what was most meaningful to them was not their aptitude, their positions, or their earnings, but the people they loved. It's a timeless lesson.

" It's important to think about human connections: what are we doing for the people in our lives? "

Chris Baréz-Brown, creative and business beatnik

WHAT DO PEOPLE HAVE THAT'S REALLY WORTH WANTING?

Believing that you're not successful leads to the trap of looking at other people and drawing conclusions about what makes them successful and satisfied. There's no need to do that. We recommend you find out what really is at the heart of their lives. You might be surprised and inspired and approach what you want in a different way.

The *World Happiness Report,*[6] which has been published annually since 2012, covers 158 countries. The report doesn't confine itself to money as a measure of a society's wellbeing. It also assesses healthy life expectancy, having someone to count on, perceived freedom to make life choices, freedom from corruption and generosity. The analysis of the results, which are featured widely in the media, comes from a variety of experts ranging from economists to neuroscientists. In 2015 it was clear that our wellbeing was influenced by our individual family and friendships, as well as our trust in our community and society.

> **"We have these phrases like 'gut feeling' and 'in my heart' which tell us what we really want; we need to quieten the noise in our head and listen downwards."**
>
> Kele Baker, mind-body-movement coach

DANNIE-LU CARR ON WANTING THE EXTERNAL VALIDATION FIX

'Everywhere we turn we're told in one way or another that money, and what money can buy, validates us. So we think a bag or a technology item can add some sort of value to us. These messages are around us subliminally everywhere so we don't even realize we're doing this. Of course we all love nice things – but we need to do a lot of work on ourselves to make sure we don't rely on these, that things don't become the fix.

There are times when guidance is necessary to work all this out. This guidance can come through a friend, a therapist, a coach. There are times when you need the courage to look at yourself and admit you're not happy, this bag isn't making you happy, this new gadget isn't making you happy. Yes, this is terribly hard to face.

Shopping is a fix – it's a hit, but it doesn't last. It's instant gratification. It's a sticking plaster, but it doesn't heal the problem.

Checking in with ourselves is hard. Our bodies give us the clues. Feeling tired, drained, constantly unwell, suffering from knots in the stomach, are all signs that our instant gratification system isn't working.'

THE MYTH OF FAME AND FORTUNE

There's no escaping the words fame and fortune in a discussion about ambition and success. Regardless of whether having fame and fortune is something that you want or not, there's no ignoring news about celebrities, and that includes all the stories of addiction, depression and broken relationships. But let's move away from entertainment stars to people who achieve the kind of fame that is more about recognition, those people who achieve a higher than average wealth. Are they good role models for ambition and success?

Certainly there are people in this category whose stories will give you lessons in achieving status and wealth goals. We want to go beyond this though. Rather than asking you what you think status and wealth will give you, we've turned to the research that has asked these questions of people who have it all. One of the most fascinating studies on the subject is a landmark study[7] by three University of Rochester researchers which demonstrated that having money and fame doesn't lead to happiness.

The study confirmed that the greater the commitment to a goal, the more likelihood of success. However, the findings departed from previous studies in discovering that there isn't a correlation with happiness. In fact, the study showed that materialistic and 'image-related' goals contributed to negative symptoms (like shame and anger) rather than positive wellbeing. On the other hand, individuals with goals based on health and personal growth, relationships and community involvement were more satisfied with achieving these, experienced far less stress and had higher levels of wellbeing.

The authors pointed to the need for 'psychologically nourishing experiences', like being with friends or having a hobby. They also highlighted that wanting money and adoration breeds inadequacy and jealousy.

If a fantasy about money and adoration becomes a picture of what you *think* you want, it can stop you figuring out what it is you *do* want – and (as we discover later in Chapter 9) that's an obstacle to ambition and success.

BUY EXPERIENCES

A series of surveys[8] over several years by assistant professor of psychology Leaf Van Boven at the University of Colorado concluded in 2003 that people from all socioeconomic backgrounds are happier when they spend on experiences rather than material goods.

Rather than dreaming about what you want, find a way to experience something you want right now. If you want to have fun, then consider what you can do within your financial circumstances that's fun now. Instead of buying clothes or technology, buy an afternoon, evening or day to remember. Investigate experiences that go beyond what you normally and routinely do.

Psychologists have known for some time that fame and fortune are not real wants based on what we need as human beings to thrive. The leading authority on the subject is Edward Deci who is Professor of Psychology and Gowen Professor in Social Sciences at the University of Rochester. He's also the director of the university's human motivation programme. Deci and his colleagues have been studying motivation since the fifties.

Two of the authors of the above study, Deci and psychologist Richard Ryan, developed the Self-Determination Theory on human motivation. They found through their research that motivation to get what we want is based on meeting the psychological needs for autonomy, competence and relatedness (connection). We want to be free to make decisions for ourselves (autonomy), we want to feel capable in all areas of our lives (competence), and we need to matter to others, to love and be loved (connectedness). All the research since supports this theory. Wanting to be rich and famous doesn't fit in with the basic human psychological needs. (In fact, in Chapter 6 you'll discover that the illusion of needing this is a major trap and an obstacle to success.)

Understanding where motivation comes from, what it's really about, and how it fits in with your wants and needs is like being your own inner detective. One of the biggest mysteries is why you might feel a need to pursue something, whether it's working for yourself, getting promoted or following a particular career, for example. Discovering what drives you is fascinating.

WHAT DRIVES YOU?

If success is the destination and ambition is the vehicle, drive is the satnav with a will of its own. Ideally you want the bossiest inner satnav that will get you there no matter what. For the moment let's consider what's behind the drive to do something in particular.

Daniel H. Pink's book *Drive*[9] looks at the 'mismatch between what science knows and what business does'. Pink holds up Wikipedia, the largest encyclopedia, as an example that illustrates conventional business approaches to motivation. Wikipedia, points out Pink, is written entirely by volunteers who don't have a boss and aren't driven by a (financial) reward. According to Pink the 'carrot and stick' works for certain types of work but not anything that involves thinking or creativity (and by creativity that includes problem solving). 'Intrinsic motivation is conducive to creativity,' he writes. Routine jobs, he explains, need direction, but interesting jobs need self-direction.

Think about that last line and take it further. It's not just interesting jobs that need self-direction, it's interesting lives. If you want to be rewarded quickly for what you think you want to do, your inner satnav will play up. External rewards are not the key to firing up your motivation. This isn't news to psychologists. Deci first researched and wrote about this in the seventies.[10]

We might laugh at the cliché that is keeping up with the Jones's. We don't need academic studies to tell us the obvious, do we? People can't help looking at what other people have, and don't want to be left behind. Anthropologists are all too aware of this. In *Time Magazine*'s cover story on ambition in 2005[11] anthropologist Edward Lowe at Soka University of America referred to 'status anxiety'. 'Whether you're born to be concerned about it or not, you do develop it,' he told the magazine.

When we consider that there are entire industries devoted to making us want items, it's worth asking why we make those choices that don't really matter: the gadget you bought, the item of clothing, the car, the trainers. If everyone's buying a Nutribullet juicer or a spiralizer you can be fooled into thinking you need these. Maybe you do – maybe you don't. Some items will be with you for years, and others will just sit there. Hey, what does it matter? It matters when you get swept along in the same way about how you lead your life.

WHAT'S THE *UNMET NEED* THAT DRIVES YOU?

The problem is that unless you question why you live life as you do, what is driving you and why, you won't be aware of negative beliefs that have become a big part of you. It's easy to confuse an intrinsic drive to do something positive with a negative need that drives you to do something that doesn't suit you. Author Duncan Coppock's approach to coaching[12] is based on identifying unmet emotional needs. These emotional needs go back to childhood but stay rooted in our psychological make-up because they become wired into our brain. Unless you identify the dodgy wiring, you can't rewire. Thankfully we know from neuroscience that rewiring our thoughts and beliefs is possible. Sure, it takes being conscious and working at it, but it's possible.

You might hazard a guess that any addiction can be traced to 'something else'. However, you may be unaware that working long hours without recognition, or getting fired, or never being able to last in a relationship are all examples of fulfilling an unmet need. Don't worry if this is a tricky concept to get your head round. The test at the end of this chapter will help you understand this further as well as identifying your unmet needs.

You can of course work on identifying the source of your unmet needs. If it's to feel special, perhaps you were one of many siblings. If it's to be independent, perhaps it's because your childhood was unstable and frightening. What's more important, however, is to identify what belief you formed about yourself – one that you might still be carrying with you through adulthood. Believing that you're not good enough, that you're hopeless, that everybody else gets 'it' except you, are negative beliefs that drive you all day every day. You can programme your internal satnav to go to your chosen destination, but if you get out of the car, your ambitions will be nothing but empty wishes.

Once you begin to question your unmet needs and how to meet these in a healthy way, you will inevitably find other ways to satisfy your needs. These new ways will be your real ambition – and success follows organically. Your inner needs will transform into inner goals – and you will be matching your outer goals to these.

KELE BAKER ON INNER AND OUTER GOALS

- *'Is what you want about achieving a goal or is it about wanting to be happy?*

- *Identify a specific goal and then ask yourself: Is my ambition to achieve something in the outer world or within myself?*

- *Ask yourself: What is it I want to feel inside?*

- *Think in terms of outer and inner expressions of you: the outer expression is the ambition to achieve the goal. But the question is: What is it you want to feel through achieving this? Then work from this inner feeling to find another outer expression. If that goal will make you feel important because you will be a leader, what else can you do to lead? If running your own business will make you feel independent, for example, what else can you do to feel independent?*

- *Train yourself to identify your inner desires. Ask: How can I satisfy my inner desires? If you ask with an open mind you might get an answer you don't expect.*

- *Our inner desires change so we have to adjust our ambitions. Some years you may want security and then need change. A new inner need can feel scary: Will you hold back or take the plunge to try something different?*

- *Whenever you feel stuck or find yourself at a crossroads ask yourself what at that point makes you happy. Compile a list without questioning what you write down. Make it as detailed as possible including details about your home, where you like to go, the skills you most enjoy using, the people you are drawn to.*

  Your list will guide you to opportunities by prompting your mind to take notice of opportunities to explore. You may even start to experience coincidences and synchronicity.'

We hope it's become clear that establishing what you really want involves delving deep inside to identify your needs. In this way you can form ambitions that are attainable because they are true to you. On the surface, ambition might appear to be about status and money, but real ambition goes beyond this and strikes at our inner selves.

Through our tests you will be able to investigate in more detail whether what you're truly striving for is love, acceptance, making a difference, doing what you love, being with people you love. There's nothing wrong with wanting material things, but these aren't real desires. The icing makes a cake look fabulous, but it's the cake we really want to make and it's the cake we really want to eat.

Once you click in to what your real psychological needs are you will be able to create a balanced vision of what you want to create your successful life. You'll be clear about your destination and that inner satnav will have a far easier route without conking out.

As we move away from the old-school ambition that came to mean a ruthless push for money and status (which don't equal happiness anyway), you can see that you don't need one overriding ambition to be successful. One of your reasons for buying this book may have been not knowing what that one ambition is so that you can achieve success. Now you know from the research that we've presented that true success in terms of wellbeing and life satisfaction is multidimensional. And if you do have 'one thing' you're driven to achieve, you also know now that success in terms of wellbeing and life satisfaction doesn't come from that 'one thing' alone.

REAL PEOPLE

"I didn't realize my ambition covered up my shame." – *Annabel*

'Everyone says I shouldn't complain because I've got what I wanted and what so many women want: a successful man who provides an amazing lifestyle for me as a woman, our two children, and us as a family. I never realized until recently that what I wanted was unhealthy. It was about making up for the shame I felt as a child about my family not having money and not doing very well.

When I was a young solicitor I had no interest in being a successful lawyer and having a career. I didn't want to be a partner in a firm, I wanted to marry one. That was my ambition: to marry an ambitious man. My friends at the time were focusing on their careers. I didn't approve of the men they got into relationships with because prestige and prospects were what mattered to me. I was conscious that I didn't want to be like my mum, always worrying about money because my dad was useless with no ambition. I didn't understand though until recently that my feelings about my parents affected my self-esteem.

I fell in love with my husband when we both joined the same legal firm as juniors. I put my energy into helping my husband achieve his ambitions as soon as we were in a committed relationship. I thought I was investing in us. In fact I was satisfying my unmet needs to be better than everyone else. I handled our finances, and planned for us financially, from buying our first property with the help of his family, to moving up. I made sure he ate healthily, and even when I still worked full time I spent Sundays cooking home-made meals for the week. We had children when we could afford for me to give up working. By this stage he was partner of a major firm. But with that came more responsibility. I had two toddlers and was exhausted and he was jet setting around Europe and going out for fancy dinners. I resented it.

The arguments got worse. I felt like a glorified housekeeper even though we had a cleaner and au pair to help. I lost touch with my friends. Actually I fell out with a couple. I felt they were judgemental though, looking back, I can see I was judgemental of them but also envious of their independence. But I was no different to my mum: unhappy. I covered it up for sake of our two boys. I was proud they got into the best schools. I was ambitious for them too.

Thankfully, I didn't just marry an ambitious man, but a good man too, who refused to let us divorce unless we had counselling and therapy. He read a lot on planes and was interested in living a meaningful, conscious life and I began to read these books too. I am grateful that we are together and now the boys are at university we are spending more time together. But I am also spending more time on me, discovering who I am for the first time in my life. Through therapy I've had to really explore my childhood and how this has affected me in adulthood. Understanding what should have been obvious has been a relief. I am grateful for the wonderful family I have in my life. Now I can work on feeling good about myself.'

ASK YOURSELF

Q I want ... because ...?

Q I need ... to ...?

Q I need ... because ...?

Q What gets in the way of me doing what I really want do is ...?

Q The difference between what I want and what I need is ...?

Q I think about what I want in relation to...?

Q But I've never thought about what I want in terms of ...?

Q What are the things I want to *do* every day?

Q What are the feelings I need to *feel* every day?

WHAT ARE YOUR UNMET NEEDS?

And how can you get them met in a healthy way?

Do your fantasies of success change on weekly basis? Have you ever felt flat after achieving a goal you'd worked hard for? Or held back from pursuing a goal because of other people's reactions? If so, chances are you have unmet needs that are hijacking your ambition. We all strive for success for different reasons, but we can run into problems when our motivation is driven by an unmet need, whether that's for attention, security or validation. But by becoming aware of these often powerful subconscious drives, you increase your chances of setting the right goals, and investing your energy in the right direction. It's time to get to know the most important person in your life – yourself!

Test by Sally Brown

QUESTION 1

You get into the lift with your boss at work and they barely acknowledge you. Do you:

A. Shrug it off – they must have a lot on their mind.

B. Feel indignant – how dare they humiliate you in public like that?

C. Panic and wonder if they're thinking about sacking you.

D. Fight back tears – you know it's silly but you feel hurt.

QUESTION 2

What was the main reason for leaving your last job?

A. I was worried the company was going to close.

B. I wanted a job with a higher profile.

C. I didn't like the dynamic in the office – I always felt like an outsider.

D. It was time for a new challenge.

QUESTION 3

What would be (or has been) the hardest part of being unemployed for you?

A. Staying motivated and positive about applying for jobs.

B. Not knowing how to reply when someone asks me what I do for a living.

C. The stress of unpaid bills and mounting debts.

D. Spending most of the day on my own.

QUESTION 4

What is most likely to put you in a good mood?

A. Paying the bills for the month ahead and still having money left over.

B. A good night's sleep or doing some exercise.

C. Being invited to a group social event.

D. Being notified that someone important has viewed my LinkedIn profile.

QUESTION 5

When scanning job ads, what's most likely to catch your eye?

A. Something that would make the most of my skills and talents.
B. Jobs with better pay.
C. A small company that sounds friendly.
D. An impressive job title.

QUESTION 6

A very successful friend tells you that they've just left their job to set up a small business. You feel:

A. Pleased, but you also wonder if they'll have as much time for you.
B. Pleased for them and hope they do well.
C. Bemused that they could leave a top job to start again at the bottom.
D. In awe – even the thought of doing it yourself makes you feel anxious.

QUESTION 7

A new neighbour moves in. Apart from welcoming them to the neighbourhood, what would be your main motivation for calling on them?

A. To find out if they're going to be a nightmare neighbour.
B. To see if I could help in any way.
C. To see if they could be a potential new friend.
D. To fill them in on my various roles in the community.

QUESTION 8

In a relationship, what's the 'type' you'd most like to end up with?

A. Hardworking, successful, and well-connected.
B. Down-to-earth, reliable and good with money.
C. It varies – whoever shows a real interest in me.
D. Someone with a good sense of humour and zest for life.

Now, add up your scores from each answer using the following table, and find out how your unmet needs are influencing your success:

	A	B	C	D
Q1	4	2	1	3
Q2	1	2	3	4
Q3	4	2	1	3
Q4	1	4	3	2
Q5	4	1	3	2
Q6	3	4	2	1
Q7	1	4	3	2
Q8	2	1	3	4

If you scored between 8 and 13 ...

You crave security

You often feel anxious about the future and, at times, you can get fixated on money, feeling that all your problems would be solved if you had more. There are times in everyone's life when money worries are a real concern. The difference is that you don't feel relaxed about your future even when your bank balance is healthy – you spend a lot of time in 'what if' mode, and a problem at work can trigger a fantasy about becoming jobless, penniless and homeless. In evolutionary terms, our need to feel safe and secure is one of our strongest drives. If security was elusive or inconsistent in your childhood, you can grow up with your 'threat radar' stuck on alert-mode. In terms of your ambition, it can make stepping out of your comfort zone simply feel too uncomfortable, holding you back from reaching your true potential. Rewiring an anxious brain starts with being more self-compassionate and understanding towards yourself. Then try making small changes to your daily routine, like taking a different route to work. It can show you that you *can* survive and even thrive on change.

If you scored between 14 and 20 ...

You crave validation

Shaky self-belief means you can overly rely on external validation to shore up your self-esteem. That means you can be unduly influenced by what other people define as success, rather than listening to your own instincts. It may have served you well in the past, fuelling your ambition to climb the next rung of the ladder or push yourself out of your comfort zone. But the downside is it can also trap you into staying in a job that no longer truly reflects your values. You may be aware that a change in job or even career direction is overdue, but do you wonder who you'll be without the job title on your business card? Letting go of a status job is easier when you have a strong sense of self. Connecting with your personal strengths can be a useful first step – take a free test devised by positive psychologist Martin Seligman to help identify yours at www.viacharacter.org.

If you scored between 21 and 27 ...

You crave attention

Your strongest drive is to be the centre of attention, and it may be one that got you into trouble at school for being the joker or a troublemaker. Whether you felt ignored in a large family or by parents who seemed to have more important priorities in life than you, there's a 'little you' inside that is still jumping up and down and demanding attention. If creating drama worked for you as a child, you may still be working that dynamic as an adult, with your friends and colleagues roped in as an unwilling audience. Or you may have strong people-pleasing tendencies, constantly trying to mould your personality to be what you feel other people want. Both of these responses can hinder your career development and stop you being taken seriously by other people. Developing your self-compassion is a powerful way to soothe your inner child. Try a book like Paul Gilbert's *The Compassionate Mind*.

If you scored between 28 and 32 ...

Your needs are well-met

You may have done a lot of work on your personal issues, or been lucky to grow up naturally well-balanced, stable and secure. Either way, your authentic passions and interests are in the driving seat of your ambition rather than your unmet needs. You're in the ideal place to stop, step back and take an objective look at your future plans. Read on for more guidance on finding out what ambition means to you, and how to achieve it.

CHAPTER 3

HOW DOES REAL AMBITION FEEL?

Our modern society certainly has a number of problems, like high stress, increasing numbers of people suffering from depression and anxiety, and terminal diseases like cancer. However, one of the advantages of modern society is that there is no norm. Achieving success is more attainable because there really is no set path. In previous eras, success might have meant overcoming being female, or being poor, or having a child out of wedlock. All of the key battles for freedom in this country have pretty much been won.

The more accurate question is: How does real success feel to *you*? At some point in your life you will have experienced a sense of success in something. It may have been a feeling of satisfaction when you accomplished something at school or when you were a child. When you begin to investigate yourself and trace back these feelings, however fleeting or brief they were, you will be able to then trace your bespoke route to success.

" If you get your energy aligned and are doing all the right stuff for you, then there's an effortless feeling to creating success. "

Chris Baréz-Brown, creative and business beatnik

DESIGNING A LIFE AROUND YOUR VALUES

In the last chapter, we explained that pursuing ambitions based on unmet needs isn't real ambition. Through our test you will have identified your own unmet needs which will enable you to find healthy ways to fulfil these. The exciting bit about real ambition is designing our lives around our values. Your values are a combination of what is meaningful to you and what excites you.

Think of the difference between needs and values as the difference between foods you crave and foods that give you zest and energy. Behind every craving there's a nutritional need, but unless we know this and look after ourselves we'll scoff the crisps or the sweets. When we're looking after ourselves we know that certain foods boost both our bodies and mind. It's the same with values: these are the healthy pursuits you're drawn to that make you feel positive, hopeful, excited and full of energy.

If you've been in a rut or your self-esteem has taken a bashing it's natural to feel that it's not possible to live life according to what you love. After all, if you've been made redundant and have financial problems, for example, it's understandable that you feel despondent. However, injecting your life with your values in any way is what will help you become hopeful again. If your value is creativity, for example, you can start writing or painting right now.

As far as your career is concerned, headhunter and coach John Purkiss believes it's essential to identify your values. They will help you to know which types of work are right for you and which are not. 'Two people with identical talents but dissimilar values are likely to pursue entirely different careers,' write Purkiss and David Royston-Lee in *Brand You*.[1]

The self-awareness you gain from knowing yourself and being crystal clear about what matters most to you gives a certain confidence: 'You become like a magnet, attracting people who hold similar values.'[2]

The key to outlining your values is going within. Rather than focusing on what gives you instant gratification (as that might be driven by an unmet need) pay attention to what you feel strongly about. Ask yourself: In what way would incorporating this in your life make you feel satisfied and bring out the best in you? When you match your values to your actions you are truly bound for success.

A TRUE INNER MATCH

In a society and culture where there are boundless choices, choice creates its own problems. Too much choice can leave you overwhelmed. The challenge is to find all the elements that you, and only you, need in your life, so that you, and only you, feel good. And it is a challenge. Even people who know from a young age that they want to sing or dance or act or write still have to figure out *how*, and they still have to figure out what else they need. You need a true inner match in all areas of your life.

> **"Living from the inside out means learning about your deeper truths and joys and following that path."**
>
> Kele Baker, mind-body-movement coach

Imagine you want to set up a business, and you even have in mind the type of business. Maybe you're at the stage of wondering whether it's a dream, whether you've got what it takes, whether you're shooting for the stars. Let's say life delivers you a mentor who helps you set up your business. The problem is, if you haven't also thought about your friendships, your family, what kind of love relationship you want, your health, your entertainment and downtime, where you want to live, it's possible that somewhere along the line there will be a block. You might set up the business in record time, but feel lonely. You might work long hours and get ill before the business takes off. You might tick off business goals, bank balance, own home, but feel a strange emptiness that has to be filled with alcohol or any relationship to save you from being alone. Is that a life you want?

❝The more you pay attention to and prioritize who you really are and what you love, the more you can let life unfold, and the more success flows.❞

Kele Baker, mind-body-movement coach

When everything in your life is aligned, life falls into place. If you're experiencing inner and outer chaos right now this might seem like an impossible concept, so let's describe it in a different way. Let's say you've been trying out 'simple' pasta recipes that are in fact a big faff because of all the pots and pans you've got to set up and then wash up, not to mention getting hold of all the ingredients. Then, by chance, you find a recipe for that one-pot pasta dish that's quick, easy, delish and perfect the day after for packed lunch. This is what you're aiming for in life too – a recipe for life that works for you.

 ## FOCUS ON ONE TASK AT A TIME

In a fast-moving modern lifestyle, you've probably been led to believe that multi-tasking is a great thing. It's become the norm now: people are on the mobile phones having a conversation while doing something routine on their computer and even keeping an eye on social media. Creativity specialist Dannie-Lu Carr recommends working hard for intense periods of time and building in time to rest and refocus instead.

When this happens, there's space in your life to surprise yourself because you will have a sound foundation from which to make changes. It's very common for people to feel that if they don't know what their one ambition is, this means they are not ambitious. Many people also feel that if they don't even have an interest or hobby they are passionate about, then they can't summon up whatever is needed to be successful.

By making even tiny changes in all areas of your life, however, you will help yourself find the big changes. If you're in a rut it's understandable that you feel overwhelmed about how to get out. But just taking a different route to work, eating a different lunch, having a shower in the evening instead of the morning – any change in your routine – helps to lubricate the wheels for bigger changes. The point about making small and seemingly insignificant changes is that you won't be questioning or judging them. And that's the space you need to be in to find the courage to take the leaps in your life. Think of that sense you have when you dive into an azure swimming pool or squeal your way into the sea. It's an intoxicating mix of intention and spontaneity.

> **" Malala went from a tiny village in North West Pakistan and speaking up against the Taliban, to becoming a world-famous advocate of women's education and winning the Nobel Peace Prize. You couldn't plan that. "**
>
> John Purkiss, headhunter and coach

FINDING YOUR CORE CALLING

Could anyone have predicted the craze for adult colouring books? At the end of 2015, Amazon's top 20 bestsellers included three colouring books. Did Millie Marotta[3] (whose first colouring book became a phenomenal success) mastermind the craze that became a form of mindfulness? She was an illustrator who was approached with the idea because the publishers loved her work and believed she would be ideal. She was the perfect match.

When you find your inner calling you become a match for something out there – that can't be planned. You probably know at least one person who has always 'known' what they wanted to do. That person might even be lucky enough to be doing this successfully. Successfully, in this sense, has come to be associated with doing the 'one thing' as a career, earning a salary and recognition from it. We hope through this book that we might encourage you to go beyond believing that something is only a success if it's a career, and that ambition is only about career. Real ambition is knowing your true desires and making these happen so that you live a fulfilled – successful – life. It's possible to have passions that have nothing to do with your career or what you do to pay your bills – and it's also possible that your calling in life has nothing to do with what you do for a living, a hot-shot career, or even a hobby you're passionate about.

The idea that we have a central calling goes back to Swiss psychiatrist and psychoanalyst Carl Jung, who developed his theories in the fifties. Professor of Psychology and licensed clinical psychologist Lisa Fortlouis Wood explains that according to Jung each of us has a unique calling and it's through this that we contribute to the world at large. 'Jung's philosophy is about each person creating and actualizing their own calling by tapping into who they are, their own internal experience,' she explains.

So does this mean that if you're hell-bent on singing for a living and becoming a pop star that you should pursue your ambition because that's your calling? It depends. Knowing your calling doesn't guarantee success in terms of recognition or getting paid. It's the beginning of the process. The process may take many years of hard work, but that doesn't mean you have to jeopardize or put the rest of your life on hold. 'Many people do give up material things to make things happen,' says Professor Fortlouis Wood. 'But this isn't about starving on the street.'

Healthy success certainly isn't about deluding yourself. You may know someone who has a thing about doing something in particular, and it might be obvious to all except this very person that it's not very good for them. They might refuse to do any work other than their dream job, or they might refuse to date anyone with less than a certain bank balance.

Let's say for the moment you don't have a job, and your dream meal would be at the top restaurant in the world because being a foodie is your calling, food is your passion. At the time of writing the top restaurant in the world is El Celler de Can Roca in Girona, Spain.[4] There's a one year waiting list and it costs €300 to eat there. Does this mean you can't be a real foodie until and unless you get here? Will it still be number one when you can afford to go there? And, if not, what if the next top restaurant is one that's even more expensive? If you have a passion for food you know very well that whether you can or can't go to a certain destination is no mark of your passion. Did having no money stop food blogger Jack Monroe[5] from cooking? No. It inspired a blog on cooking on a budget which led to a book deal and media columns.

FIND YOUR MOST ABSORBING EXPERIENCES

You may have heard of the concept of 'flow', which was coined in the seventies by Hungarian Holocaust survivor Mihaly Csikszentmihalyi.[6] When people have their most satisfying experiences, time flies by because they are completely absorbed. Conversely, when these experiences are taken away, people become anxious and tired. With this in mind, start to monitor when you lose track of time. Which activities create flow in your life? Which activities absorb you so much you don't check your phone incessantly, in fact you don't even hear it? When you can't do these activities, what's the effect on your body and mind? Absolutely any activity counts: be prepared to be surprised.

The more you know yourself as a person, the more you can arrive at what you believe is at your core. It can be as simple as making people laugh or showing your love through baking, or as challenging as gaining a political position to make a difference in government. You might not know exactly what this is. For example, you might have an amazing singing voice, but feel you're not cut out to be a pop star, yet feel confused because you want to sing every day. Well, maybe your calling *is* to sing, but not necessarily as a pop star. Maybe you'll set up a community choir that makes money for a charity that's close to your heart. Maybe you'll study singing and become a vocal-coach for leading singers. Patsy Rodenburg OBE (one of our experts in our book *Real Confidence*) started out with a calling for drama, yet didn't want to be an actress. She became one of the world's leading authorities on voice, training A-list stars in theatre and film, a leading authority on Shakespeare and a leadership coach.

Being self-aware and assessing your psychological make-up in relation to the one thing you love will lead you to a channel for that passion. This will be a channel that suits you, so you'll feel totally comfortable. As a result you will be in an environment that helps you thrive. By thriving you will attract and create success. An indoor plant is no lesser a plant in the plant kingdom just because it doesn't want to be outside. Yet all too often people abandon what they love because their view of this love is too narrow.

> **❝Success is being present, truthful, having integrity and making a difference to others and yourself. ❞**
>
> Dannie-Lu Carr, creativity specialist, communications consultant & creative practitioner

FREEDOM TO LIVE THE WAY YOU WANT – AND THE COURAGE TO FIND THE PLACE TO DO SO

One of the problems with having a lot of choice available is finding the courage to change what has become a routine. You have to try something or some place that's new, you have to experiment with trying many different things, different places, as well as different people, until you find the inner match in every dimension of your life and the true inner calling.

To feel there is a purpose and a meaning to life and to make things happen we need the right conditions. We are like plants that need the right soil, the right watering conditions, the right temperature and the right place in the light. If you have a plant in your home and it's not looking well, you instinctively move it around. The key is to do the same for you. When you place yourself in the ideal conditions for you, you thrive.

Successful people don't think about what other people think. We're not talking old-style ambition and success here because our interest is *balanced* success, one that's based on all the elements of life falling into place and working together. For this to happen, you may need to put yourself in the right place with the right people. If you're investigating and discovering yourself, you want to be somewhere where it's possible to experiment without anyone commenting. 'You need to be somewhere where you can drop your inhibitions,' says Purkiss.

It's not that inhibitions vanish in big cities, or that leaving your home town equals leaving all your doubts behind as well. Creating your successful life is like an artist's work in progress and, as the artist, you need the right environment to feel you can take as long as you like, or dump one painting to make a sculpture instead, or take advice, or whatever you need to do, undisturbed. Purkiss, for example, was for years a headhunter in London with orthodox contacts, and then had another life of meditation and spiritual practice. He admits to agonizing over this difference until it came to him that he could present both sides of himself. Purkiss could work through these big questions in London. For somebody else the challenge might be to leave the city and go to the country to work out their own big questions. The point is: being in the right place helps everything fall into place.

> **❝ Living in a diverse city is good for ambition because you don't have to worry so much about what people think of you. ❞**
>
> John Purkiss, headhunter and coach

THE NEW SLASHERS: DAY JOB PLUS

One of the biggest traps is viewing ambition and success based only on your day job. If you really want to act/write/sing/paint/lead then a corporate life is not for you, right? Wrong. If you are insisting that you can't take on a 'proper job', yet can't stand having to subsist on student jobs when your student days are long gone, we're not going to give you a pep talk. We're just going to say: that whole idea is outdated. The world has changed. Technology has changed. And ideas and attitudes have changed. You wouldn't persist in using an out of date phone without apps, wifi and internet, so you can now ditch outdated thinking too.

In the last few years a whole different career model has evolved which provides a whole new model for success. Many people are doing more than one thing. (The editor of *Psychologies* is a magazine editor as well as a leading life coach.) Check out how people describe themselves on Twitter and you'll notice two or three 'jobs' are listed and separated with slashes. And slashes are the way to go.

> **" Risk and definition has changed. Most people I want to employ want several jobs, they don't want to be pinned down. "**
>
> Chris Baréz-Brown, creative and business beatnik

American author, journalist, speaker Marci Alboher[7] popularized the term slasher with her book *One Person/Multiple Careers: The Original Guide to the Slash Career*. Alboher, whose background is law, thoroughly researched the book with in-depth interviews and even individual CVs. She highlights that working for the same company until we retire is no longer viable anyway. A 'composite career', as she terms it, avoids the stifling, uncreative path of the single track career. Alboher encourages us to think of a career as something that provides pleasure and satisfaction, not one that is just about income.

With this composite career in mind, you don't have to struggle to do one thing for love and another thing you hate for money. You don't need to label yourself as one thing only. When supermodels set up businesses no one bats an eyelid. Being entrepreneurs doesn't take away from their original iconic status as models. We don't think Elle Macpherson[8] is desperate or a loser because she also has a lingerie business, is a photographer, and more recently became the force behind Welleco,[9] a wellness company with nutritional products. Who is to say that you can't start a business, become a photographer, and even a model in later life? (There are model agencies[10] for older women, so we didn't just pluck that out of nowhere.)

The best aspect of this development – we're not calling it a trend as we believe it's here to stay – is that it releases us from being one thing. Invariably this one thing has come to be one's career, but not in the new paradigm of success. We can have a job that pays more than the bills and also hobbies that fulfil us and make us feel alive; we can have separate career ambitions that we nurture slowly, growing them slowly; and we can have additional roles or callings or passions that have nothing to do with any form of work. Your identity doesn't have to come from one thing and that one thing certainly doesn't have to be your job.

> **"When people think in terms of freedom it's so much more satisfying; ambition and risk are in the eyes of the beholder."**
>
> Chris Baréz-Brown, creative and business beatnik

DANNIE-LU CARR ON HOW TO FEEL SUCCESSFUL RIGHT NOW

- *'Develop self-honesty by asking yourself:* Am I feeling energized and alive, or am I feeling empty? Do more of whatever makes you feel energized and alive. And dump whatever and whoever leaves you feeling empty.

- *Develop a generous spirit:* share information, links, contacts. An abundant attitude is a successful attitude. There is enough to go round for everyone.

- *Ditch making negative assumptions:* somebody's behaviour might be coming from a painful place. Successful people aren't judgemental.

- *Ban gossiping:* don't make mean comments about others. Successful people have better things to do.

- *Be generous, positive and kind to others:* successful people don't feel the need to put others down.

- *Learn to be assertive:* successful people don't stuff their emotions like mis-matched socks in a drawer or let others walk all over them.'

Once you align the real you with your ambitions, you'll find that the concept of success won't feel like a treadmill. Through developing an awareness of what you need in all areas of your life, combined with knowing what makes you light up, a logical journey will emerge. Then you can make the decisions needed and plan your journey. There may be necessary changes; it's likely that you have a lot to learn, you will have to start doing stuff to make what it is you want actually happen, and that process of doing could be uncomfortable and tiring. Success doesn't feel instant, and it's not easy in the sense that there are no obstacles. But the journey is fascinating. Overcoming the obstacles is satisfying. It's a process that feeds you rather than drains all your energy.

You may discover that your purpose in life or your calling has nothing to do with your job or making it in a competitive field – and this discovery will be liberating as your energy can go into this. If you have a passion you're very much sure about and you feel this is your overriding ambition, with this model of success your one ambition won't be at the expense of other areas in your life. You will be able to set up the other aspects of your life to help you, which will prevent you resenting that overriding passion.

ASK YOURSELF

Q Who do I know who is satisfied with more than one area in their life?

Q Who do I know who has a passion in life, but it's not their job?

Q So far my idea of success has been someone who ...?

Q Where do I need to be to create the life I want?

Q Ever since I was ... years old I wanted to ...?

Q The times in my life when I felt my best self were when I was ... ?

WHAT AMBITION WOULD MAKE YOU FEEL FULFILLED?
Find your passion

Paradoxical as it may sound, it's perfectly possible (and actually very common) to feel ambitious for success, without having clue about what you actually want to do! Do you ever feel convinced that if only you could find the right path, there would be no stopping you? One of the most effective ways of getting one step closer to identifying where you should focus all that energy and enthusiasm is by identifying your core values. Knowing what really matters to you deep down is like having a personal guiding star, making everything from decision-making to getting up in the morning feel a whole lot easier. Take this quiz to identify the values that feed your passion.

Test by Sally Brown

QUESTION 1

Imagine you spent a morning on each of the following tasks. Which one do you think would leave you feeling the most satisfied?

A. Helping brainstorm a new idea with a group of creative thinkers.

B. Attending a talk by an inspirational leader in your field.

C. Helping a vulnerable client find a solution to a long-term problem.

D. Taking part in a team-building exercise that really breaks down boundaries between your colleagues.

QUESTION 2

If you had the opportunity to go back to learning, what category of course would you be most attracted to?

A. Creative – writing, art and design, performance art, photography or acting.

B. An MBA, MSc or PhD – you'd like an intellectual challenge and to upgrade your current qualifications.

C. Caring – social work, counselling, nursing, teaching.

D. Personal growth - NLP, the Hoffman process, or anything aimed at better communication and relationships.

QUESTION 3

You're 80 and looking back at your life. What would you hope to see evidence of?

A. Fully exploring and developing my creative talents.

B. That I never stopped learning and growing as a person.

C. Going the extra mile to make a difference to those that need it.

D. Lasting and meaningful relationships with friends, colleagues and family.

QUESTION 4

If you overheard some colleagues gossiping at work, which of these comments would be most likely to upset you?

A. That you have no imagination or creativity.

B. That you are not as popular as you think you are.

C. That you're a bit of a dinosaur – stuck in the past.

D. That you're only really out for number one.

QUESTION 5

What personality traits do you find the hardest the deal with in other people?

A. Rigidity and unquestioning following of rules.

B. A closed mind and unwillingness to embrace new ideas.

C. Unkindness and lack of empathy.

D. Self-centredness and narcissism.

QUESTION 6

What do you find the most rewarding about the work you do?

A. It's an outlet for my creativity.

B. I'm learning and growing as a person all the time.

C. I feel like I'm making a difference to people who need help.

D. It's been a source of some of my closest friendships.

QUESTION 7

At an election, which policies are most likely to persuade you to take a candidate seriously?

A. Support for the arts so more people can take part on a national and local level.

B. Reducing university tuition fees and investing in research.

C. Putting more resources into housing, education and healthcare for disadvantaged people.

D. Using tax breaks and benefits to support family life and flexible working.

QUESTION 8

If a child asked you what's important in life, how would you sum it up?

A. Enjoy the beauty of the world around you.

B. Keep an open mind and never stop learning.

C. Be useful, and be kind.

D. Never take loved ones for granted.

QUESTION 9

You've inherited a large amount of money and decide to donate some to charity. What are you most likely to do?

A. Stop a local theatre, gallery or arthouse cinema from closing down.

B. Help develop an innovative technique to introduce education to repeat offenders.

C. Set up a local charity to provide low-cost counselling to people who need it most.

D. Support a charity that tackles an issue affecting a close friend or member of your family.

QUESTION 10

Which one most closely matches your personal mission statement?

A. To celebrate the beauty of life.

B. To reach my full potential.

C. To spread kindness and compassion

D. To build meaningful relationships with others.

If you have equal numbers of more than one letter, read each section that applies, as your values will include a mix of all of them.

Mainly A

Your core values centre on creativity

When you're motivated by creativity, you have an innate drive to celebrate the beauty in life, and to find an authentic way to explore ideas or express feelings, whether it's through images, movement or performance, or the written word. You may not have ever labelled it as such, but your motivation to spend time on creative projects is a form of ambition. It's important to find a way of nurturing those ideas, which may mean investigating joining a course or group outside of work. But you can also be 'creative' in business, by coming up with innovative ideas or new approaches to tackling problems. If you truly feel there is no room for creativity in your job, your goal may be to move your career in a direction that's more in line with your values. But in the meantime, you'll feel happier if you bring even a tiny bit of creativity to your working life, whether it's starting an office choir or book group, changing your screensaver to a photograph of something you've created, or simply nurturing a beautiful plant on your desk.

Mainly B

Your core values centre on lifelong learning

You're motivated by personal growth and self-development and feel the most like 'you' when you're learning new skills. You have a growth mindset approach to life – you keep an open mind and you never assume you're an expert at anything because you know there is always more that can be learned. So it's understandable that you may struggle more than most if you've been in the same job for a while, or feel like your career isn't offering any new challenges. But the upside is that you will also be more motivated than most to embark on further education and put the time and effort into getting professional qualifications that will support your ambition, by either advancing your career, or opening the door to a new one.

Mainly C

Your core values centre on compassion

You believe in going the extra mile to make the world a better place. It may be something that has always been important to you, or something that has grown in recent years, but you're convinced that the power of kindness can improve relationships and life in general, both locally and globally. You may already have found yourself drawn to a caring profession, such as social work, nursing or counselling. But your values can also be expressed in other professions. Living compassionately often goes hand-in-hand with a well-developed sense of empathy, and you may find it easy to step into another person's shoes. This can be expressed in the corporate world in jobs that rely on building trust and good relationships with clients. If your job is at odds with this core value, then look to nurture it outside of work, perhaps in voluntary work.

Mainly D

Your core values centre on building relationships

You're the sort of person who naturally networks without even realizing you're doing it. You find other people endlessly fascinating and when you meet a new person your mind immediately starts 'joining the dots' and thinking who else you know would benefit from getting to know them. You're often at the centre of a social group, and are the 'go-to' person for organizing social events at work. Needless to say, you don't thrive when you're isolated, but you can be an asset to any working environment because you can bring a cohesive element to a disconnected group. A question to ask yourself is whether your current ambition makes the most of your innate sociability. You'll stay motivated and feel at your best if some aspect of your life regularly brings you into contact with new people.

2 WHAT'S STOPPING YOU FROM ACHIEVING YOUR AMBITIONS?

CHAPTER 4

ARE SOME PEOPLE MORE LIKELY TO SUCCEED?

Y ou may have people around you who have the knack of leading amazing, enviable lives, or you might envy people you see in the media. Whether you personally know and admire successful people or whether you envy them from a distance, it's perfectly natural to wonder if some are more cut out for success than others.

It's helpful to know whether some people are more likely to succeed and why as a way of ensuring that you're in the right psychological framework. This helps you cultivate the mindset of success. You will place yourself in life so that you are open to serendipity, luck and the thrill of randomness. To help you reach this understanding, this chapter analyses why some people are more likely to succeed so that you can maximize your ability to attract success.

KNOW YOURSELF

Let's say you're someone who gets stressed about daily deadlines, gets nervous and sensitive about office hierarchies and has strong political values. If your ambition is to work in the newsroom of a daily newspaper, it's going to be difficult to achieve this. You'll have to work to stressful deadlines, accept the hierarchy, as well as the newspaper's political line which may or may not be compatible with yours. But as we saw in the previous chapter, there's no need to abandon a calling just because you don't fit the most obvious way of following it.

In this example, by being honest with yourself, you might conclude you work better when you have time to research and analyse, rather than with deadlines to produce something fast. You may also realize that you prefer more in-depth projects rather than shorter ones that are turned round fast. And if you look at your values, it could be clear that you are highly motivated about campaigning for truth. This series of realizations can take you from news journalist to a host of other possibilities. You could head up a charity's news website, set up a blog campaigning for an issue you feel strongly about, freelance for national newspapers and specialist press – you might choose one of these options or even find a way to combine them all.

Something as basic as knowing whether you're an introvert or extrovert (and to what degree), or a combination of both, can inform your ambitions and the likelihood of success. CEOs, for example, tend to be extroverts, and as Professor of Psychology and licensed clinical psychologist Lisa Fortlouis Wood explains one of the central traits of extroverts is bringing their goals to fruition and manifesting this outwardly. 'Introverts who have an ambition may not necessarily be able to externalize it. But they may collaborate with an extrovert. CEOs are often extroverts, and their number two will complement them.'

" People who get to the top don't waste time waiting for the right moment to start. Don't wait. "

John Purkiss, headhunter and coach

Knowing yourself isn't about damning yourself. It's simply understanding how your internal system operates and how you function outwardly in different environments. Let's take the research on your place in the family. We know from psychologists and their research that the oldest child tends to be the most ambitious. A 2014 study by the Institute of Social and Economic Research[1] at the University of Essex found oldest children, especially girls, are the most ambitious, and that the wider the gap between siblings, the greater the chances of achieving a higher qualification. It may be useful to be aware of this to perhaps understand why your oldest sibling might appear to be the driven one, for example, and to let yourself off the hook. (You might also see the down side of your eldest sibling being on the receiving end of more expectations from your parents and suffering as a result.) The point is not to take this as conclusive evidence that if you are not the oldest child you can't be ambitious. For example, Madonna, seen as an ambitious woman, is a middle child.

> **"Some people have a strong drive or calling very early on, so they can make use of an education system or environment that isn't particularly encouraging through self-discovery and experimentation."**
>
> Lisa Fortlouis Wood, Professor of Psychology and licensed clinical psychologist

SHINE THROUGH YOUR INTELLIGENCE, NOT YOUR CONNECTIONS

Some people do indeed have the right connections but there's absolutely no point in dwelling on this and feeling bitter. This might help *them* through the door, but there is research[2] that shows intelligence is a more accurate predictor of success than socioeconomic background and connections. Professor Yoav Ganzach at the University of Tel Aviv studied survey data on 12,868 Americans between 1979 and 2004 covering interviews on their promotions and earnings. The participants were tracked over 25 years.

A wealthy, well-connected family can place their family members in plum jobs, but they can't control their progress from then on. With this in mind, let go of any thoughts along the lines of not knowing the 'right' people and instead look to make an impression through your abilities.

INNER MOTIVATION LASTS ALL THE WAY TO SUCCESS

Author Daniel Pink's premise in his book *Drive*[3] is that 'the carrot and stick' reward-based approach in business doesn't work. 'Intrinsically motivated people usually achieve more than their reward-seeing counterparts,' he writes, with one caveat: not in the short term. To be successful in most areas involves what psychologists refer to as mastery. And mastering anything takes time. As human beings we are genetically set up to master our environments from the moment we learn to walk as toddlers. Instinctively we know as babies that we have to get up and fall down and get up again until we can balance, and that we're likely to fall down again as we learn to balance for longer and eventually experience the thrill of walking.

Adults, particularly in our current culture, develop the misconception that ambition and success come quick and easy. Yet when it comes down to it, ambition and success are about mastering what's needed to achieve a certain goal effectively. Pink refers to mastery as 'achievement over the long haul'. To last the course, however, you need to *really* want something from within. Contrary to what we've been led to believe, wanting to be rewarded financially is not enough to keep us going. The leading psychologists[3] who research motivation consistently confirm that the motivation has to be 'intrinsic'. This type of ambition also benefits one's wellbeing. It's not the go-go-go propelled by financial rewards that can then lead to health problems.

> **" Successful people tend to be unconventional, often going beyond expectations into new areas. They break through the norms. They don't play it safe. "**
>
> Lisa Fortlouis Wood, Professor of Psychology and licensed clinical psychologist

Another myth is that doing what you love is 'easy' and leads to success. But this assumption leads only to frustration. You might want to cook/sing/write/act/lead/run every day; you might feel at your happiest doing your one chosen thing and it might be the one thing you've decided is the real inner you. What successful people know is that there is always a process of learning, trying things out, finding one's way over time.

Psychology studies[4] over a number of decades have shown that successful people *believe* success is possible because they are open to learning and they are motivated to achieve their goals stage by stage.

In our first book, *Real Confidence*, we referred to professor of psychology at Stanford University, Carol Dweck,[5] who developed the theory of mindset. Some people have a fixed mindset and believe they are the way they are (which might be lacking in confidence, lacking in ambition, unable to be successful). Others have what Dweck terms a growth mindset. They believe it's possible to change, to learn – to master a skill, to gain confidence, to take the steps towards success. Of course the crucial element required here is effort. Some people achieve their ambitions because they make the effort to do so – because the ambitions really matter to them.

TALENT ISN'T ENOUGH

Though we're not advocating a lifestyle that's based only on relentless work, we're not saying successful people achieve their ambitions without effort and hard graft. Even for people who are gifted the process isn't instant. To get good at something requires practice. To master anything – from baking bread to becoming an opera singer, from finance to science, lipsticks to politics – effort is essential. One of the most respected authorities on motivation, drive and willpower is Swedish psychologist and Conradi Eminent Scholar and Professor of Psychology at Florida State University, Anders Eriksson.[6] He researched what's termed 'deliberate practice' and it's more than likely you have come across what Eriksson wrote: 'many characteristics once believed to reflect innate talent are actually the result of intense practice extended for a minimum of 10 years.'

66 Do what you love and what you're great at. If you dream you can't quit. 99

Chris Baréz-Brown, creative and business beatnik

As creativity specialist Dannie-Lu Carr points out, we don't always know the stories behind people achieving their ambitions and attaining huge success. Sometimes it's because they conceal their vulnerability and what they went through to achieve their ambitions. Sometimes it's because people see what they want to see – and the myth of quick success seems more alluring. 'Brad Pitt didn't come out of nowhere as an actor,' says Carr who is a former actress herself. 'When you look at his audition tapes you can see how he developed. He too made his mistakes and worked hard.' In fact, one of Brad Pitt's first jobs was dressing up as a chicken for restaurant El Pollo Loco.[7]

Getting good at something takes time and involves putting in the hours required. People who achieve their ambitions find the time to do so. 'People don't realize that musicians, for example, practise for several hours a day to get good,' says Professor Fortlouis Wood. 'A lot of creative people working on their skills continue to do so for decades – it's what matters most to them so they're not attending to conventional middle-class achievements.'

This awareness of time and effort needed of course requires another quality – perseverance.

TRUE GRIT PAVES THE WAY

One of the most exciting areas of current research in psychology is perseverance. Why do some people persevere while others give up? We know from Dweck's work that people with a growth mindset believe they can learn and change any situation. Based on Dweck's theories, people who achieve their ambitions are not people who see failure as fixed. If there's a hiccup along the way, they tend not to see it as failure, they continue with their growth mindset.

"Many entrepreneurs are dyslexic. They hire people who aren't."

John Purkiss, headhunter and coach

But what exactly keeps these people going? Angela Duckworth's work at the Duckworth Lab, University of Pennsylvania,[8] has explored this. What has emerged from her studies is the concept of grit. Grit, as defined by Duckworth, is passion plus perseverance for long-term goals. 'Grit is the tendency to sustain interest in and effort toward very long-term goals.'[9]

> **❝Some people fulfil their desires because they are able to assess and deal with obstacles. ❞**
>
> Kele Baker, mind-body-movement coach

And no, talent doesn't bestow grit or trump any problems along the way. What Duckworth and her colleagues have found is that gritty people are motivated to find happiness through activities that totally absorb them and give them a sense of meaning or purpose rather than pleasure. Gritty people are also more optimistic.[10] They believe they'll get there.

Part of the research related to grit is the study of self-control, what's commonly known as willpower. If you sense that you lack grit and the willpower to develop it, what's reassuring is that it is possible to change. This can happen organically through life experience.

The plus side of downs is that you can eventually get over them and learn from them. The downs can also take you to territories you might enjoy even more. Carr was unhappy with the knocks she got as an actress. 'I felt pushed back because of physical criticisms – you're not tall enough, pretty enough. I stopped enjoying it.' Yet she didn't want to give up her love for acting, so she trained to coach actors and moved into directing. When she had to face up to financial reality and earning more money, instead of walking away from what she loved she realized that much of what she was teaching actors applied just as much in a work environment. 'Becoming a coach was exciting as I didn't have to leave what I was doing and loved. I found something else I loved that I could do alongside everything else.'

True grit isn't about making yourself miserable about persevering, it's about persevering and dealing with obstacles so that you can do what you love.

> **" In the archetypal hero's journey there is demand for adaptability and having the end goal in mind. More often than not things happen in a circuitous rather than linear route. "**
>
> Kele Baker, mind-body-movement coach

CHRIS BARÉZ-BROWN ON FINDING YOUR WAY THROUGH SCREWING UP

- *'You can't win at everything and be good all the time and be in control. Successful people know this.*

- *You can't think your way to 10 out of 10. More often than not it's likely that you'll hit 6, you learn from this and then you improve. You're likely to hit some 3s too. That's normal.*

- *Only about 10% of start-ups succeed. Successful people know this and have a "portfolio approach" to different things. If one thing doesn't work, they move on. That's life. Success involves being right in the thick of it including getting things wrong, making mistakes and screwing up badly. So you have to detach from other people observing from an armchair and making unhelpful comments.'*

REAL PEOPLE

"I channel my ambition into dangerous sports." *– Julianne*

'I'm pretty pleased about life right now. I'm not saying it's perfect, but then again I don't know if perfect exists for more than one experience at a time. When I've made it to the top of a mountain and the view is glorious, that's a pretty perfect feeling. When I'm having a lovely chilled time with my boyfriend without even leaving the house, that's perfect. Being aunty with my nieces, that's perfect.

When I took my first job as a paralegal assistant some people said I'd be bored. What they meant was they thought it was boring and they were holding out for some dream job. I didn't want to waste my time in my 20s doing work experience forever or bar work until some amazing job was advertised. I had expensive hobbies, and my parents weren't going to pay for these. Anyway, I enjoy what I do. I've got this geeky mind that's obsessed with detail. It's paid off, literally, because without even trying I've been promoted, headhunted even, and I get paid well. I still have to watch my money carefully. With the help of my parents who gave me a deposit I could buy a little place of my own. I manage my money so that I can pay my bills, pay for holidays and sports, save for emergencies, and buy presents for family. I can't fritter on handbags and shoes and clothes, but thankfully it's easy to look good on a budget.

I wasn't driven to be a lawyer, which was the right decision – I just don't have that confidence. But give me a diving challenge, a mountain to climb, a parachute to jump, I'm there! That's not to say it's easy, there are really tough challenges.

I've been with my boyfriend for two years. He's the complete opposite to me. He works in finance and isn't outdoorsy at all. He's massively into gourmet food – I'm a steak and chips girl! It was hard for him to get his head round me going on these trips, mostly with a bunch of blokes, so we didn't have a lovey dovey beginning because of that. There was a big shift when one of my adventure pals who is gay had a word with him. Then I suggested he came along with us for the scenery and food in Chamonix. That was a great turning point. Now we've really cracked it and we're so happy.'

We've given you some sound reasons to explain why some people may be more likely to achieve their ambitions than others. These reasons aren't so straightforward that you can apply them instantly to your life. You can't change when you were born in your family, and though it might be obvious whether you're an extrovert or introvert, many people lie in between. It can take time to find what motivates you and why, and if it's something new then mastering this takes time. You know now that life experience helps you develop resilience so you can cross out the word failure and replace it with something else like experience. In this way you will be cultivating the crucial quality that is grit.

There is indeed a balance between being open to ideas and being focused on a specific path. Sometimes what you truly love isn't obvious, sometimes you'll confuse an aptitude with passion because you've always been told you're good at maths or whatever. The main thing to remember is that successful people aren't afraid of taking a leap in a different direction.

ASK YOURSELF

Q Does your personality type suit your main ambition?

Q How much time do you devote to making your dreams reality?

Q How much time do you spend learning what you need to achieve your ambitions?

Q How much time do you give to your natural talent(s)?

Q How resilient are you?

CHAPTER 5

WHAT'S GETTING IN THE WAY OF YOUR SUCCESS?

When you feel that your life isn't successful, this can be one of the most painful things to deal with. If you're shy, for example, in time and as you get older you learn to accept this and simply avoid certain situations. If you don't earn a huge salary but love your job, you might decide that you're not that bothered about material things anyway. Even if you have hang-ups about your looks, there's so much accessible advice out there to help everyone make the most of themselves. But if it feels like you just can't make your life 'happen' no matter how hard you try, this pain is heavier to shift. It strikes at the core of who you are.

So far we have encouraged you to consider success in all areas of your life rather than associating success with just one thing that makes you money. Real ambition is about having a balanced life and that means that success is multi-dimensional. When you cultivate fulfilment in more than one area of your life you can also avoid the extreme disappointment that can come from one thing not working out the way you hoped.

You may have formed some views already about what might be getting in the way of your success. From a position of disappointment and pain people are often hard on themselves. You might be feeling you're not good enough, not confident enough, not go-getting enough. These are in fact limiting beliefs that hold you back. What's reassuring is that once you are aware of what they are, you can change them.

STAND TALL

Simply changing your posture can send messages to your brain that help you feel more confident and capable of success. Just sitting up straight and standing up without slouching – which are sound

and healthy habits for your body anyway – will make a difference to how you feel. At the same time, this will make a difference to how you are perceived. Research from the Kellogg School of Management at Northwestern University[1] found that posture plays a crucial role in coming across as successful. Having an open, 'expansive' posture was found to even trigger behavioural changes that could override a candidate's psychological position (e.g. being interviewed) so that participants could think and act more confidently. More recently, social psychologist Amy Cuddy's extensive research[2] demonstrated that just two minutes a day of putting oneself in an open posture triggers positive changes in brain chemistry. Try it.

At the other end of the scale there's a temptation to blame others. In this case you might resent your parents for depriving you of certain opportunities, or you might feel bitter about people you know who have the right contacts. Again, these thoughts are nothing but limiting beliefs you have built up over a period of time. Understanding what's getting in the way of your success isn't about laying blame on anything or anyone, and that includes yourself too.

As we saw in Chapter 4, knowing yourself is crucial. Successful people don't put themselves in situations where they're not going to thrive. Developing self-awareness means you can resolve anything that needs to be addressed, avoid anything and anyone that can be avoided, and develop an approach that benefits your process of achieving your ambitions. By knowing yourself you can also confront the limiting beliefs that are getting in your way, and by identifying what these are you can work on removing them.

"The only way to find out if a desire is a true one is by doing it, and in the doing there is learning. "

Kele Baker, mind-body-movement coach

JOHN PURKISS ON THE DANGER OF LIMITING BELIEFS

'It's very common for people to visualize what they want and then let their mind produce reasons why it isn't possible. It's important to ditch all these reasons, not your idea.

People think the reasons are realistic: "I didn't go to university, I am dyslexic, too old, too young etc." These are limiting statements. They are thought currents that run continuously in the mind and control our lives. If we believe these statements then we limit ourselves.

Believing that you can't follow your dreams because of your current circumstances or previous experiences is also limiting.'

YOUR SCHOOL DIDN'T SHOW YOU HOW TO DEVELOP AS AN INDIVIDUAL

Let's think about how we use smartphones for a moment. Perhaps you've always had a smartphone and sort of instinctively figured it out. Or maybe you had to switch and it was frustrating having to learn. Then again, you might be a technology geek who was one of the first to embrace this gadget that is now part of our everyday lives. Now think of someone older who is struggling to learn how to use a smartphone. Is it your grandparent's fault that they don't know? Of course not.

So it might surprise you to learn that what's in the way of your success is that you weren't taught how to discover what gives you a buzz and how to turn that into the basis of your life. You might not have been taught how to look at yourself in relation to all aspects of life. If you weren't able to learn while you were developing from child to adult, you can end up in a haze. Professor of Psychology and licensed clinical psychologist Lisa Fortlouis Wood (who is a specialist in both adolescence and education) highlights this issue: 'From then on [after education] people don't know how to build the process to probe their own thoughts and allow creative associations.'

> ❝**The education system doesn't encourage each individual to develop an internal evaluation system so that they learn how and when they are motivated.** ❞
>
> Lisa Fortlouis Wood, Professor of Psychology and licensed clinical psychologist

Some people, of course, have been lucky to know what motivates them from a young age. Writers, singers, actors and artists, for example, tend to 'know' very early on. But it's partly luck because from a very early age, even at nursery school, children are telling stories, singing songs, pretending in games and drawing.

What's reassuring about Professor Fortlouis Wood's analysis is her tremendous compassion. People have a hard time making it in life because society, from education to corporations, isn't favouring individual development, so inevitably people get stuck – and then blame themselves.

ASK YOURSELF

Q How did school make you feel as a child – and as a teenager? Can you identify the view(s) you formed about yourself during your school years?

Q What did teachers constantly tell you? (e.g. 'You are hopeless at maths', 'you can't pay attention', 'you never try hard enough'.) Can you see a link between these comments and your life now?

Q How many ideas do you remember absorbing about what you could do with your life? What comments (if any) from teachers inspired you to follow a career or interest?

YOUR CHILDHOOD IS DRIVING YOUR ADULTHOOD

It would be nice to be able to tell you to put aside a psychotherapy approach and to concentrate on one that's cognitive – changing your behaviour now, without dwelling on the past. But at *Psychologies* we're interested in all aspects of psychology, and while we don't like to dwell on the past, an understanding is useful. This isn't about blaming parents who didn't encourage you or teachers who were mean to you. Successful people don't blame. What's crucial here is uncovering the thought patterns and belief systems you created as a child that have stayed lodged in your mind. We know from neuroscience that the brain is capable of change, but we need to know what needs to change first, otherwise it's like trying to change a light bulb in the dark.

66 If you're told time and time again you're not good enough, you will believe it. 99

Lisa Fortlouis Wood, Professor of Psychology and licensed clinical psychologist

It's also important to acknowledge rather than deny any problems that have affected you. An American study[3] in 2015 confirmed that children suffering even mildly from depression or anxiety do have problems leading successful lives as adults. One major study[4] by Professor Fortlouis Wood (and Galena K. Rhoades at the University of Denver) found that college students who were distressed about family problems experienced difficulties in adjusting socially.

Being successful doesn't exactly mean putting aside those nagging feelings inside. Covering up these feelings takes up valuable mental energy. Uncovering them allows you to move on.

It's quite possible to forget events that continue to shape our lives decades later. If there is a big gap between your inner image (the way you see yourself) and your outer image (the way you project yourself to others), it is likely that you can trace it back to some event in your early childhood. For example, when coach John Purkiss attended a spiritual retreat with Paramahamsa Nithyananda, he realized that his inner image was 'I am unacceptable', while his outer image was 'I am clever and friendly'. He then traced this back to his early childhood: 'When I was four years old we moved from the Home Counties to Leicester where the accent was different. On my first day at school the kids laughed at me because of the way I spoke. From then onwards I felt that I was unacceptable. For many years my life was shaped by that one event. I saw myself as an outsider. I spent most of my time with other outsiders. It really limited me.'

If you take a hard look at your life, you can identify the patterns that repeat themselves, which is a starting point for undoing them. If something 'keeps happening' to you, then it isn't an accident. 'These patterns aren't random,' says Purkiss. 'If you're always falling out with people or consistently being passed over for promotion, then you are doing something that makes it happen. The same is true if you never have enough money, or keep having trouble in your relationships.'

When issues aren't addressed they simply pile up and effectively you learn to deny what hurts. Fast forward to being made redundant and feeling a mix of shame, failure, disappointment, frustration, anger, bitterness and confusion. Processing your feelings doesn't need to be complicated. It can be as simple as sharing how you feel with people who have been through a similar experience (and ideally have overcome it) or keeping a diary.

ASK YOURSELF

Q What messages about you and your future did you receive from your family? How do these relate to beliefs you have right now about yourself? (e.g. 'Don't get above yourself', 'A job is a job', 'You need security', 'Doing what you love is pie in the sky' ...)

Q Which were the trickiest periods of growing up for you? Can you see a link with tricky times now?

Q Can you identify a belief you formed in childhood about coping with difficult times? (e.g. 'Keep a stiff upper lip', 'Don't tell anyone', 'Act fine', 'No one else is like this ...')

Q How did your parents sum things up when there were problems? Do you use any of these phrases? Have any of these become your beliefs? (e.g. 'No one cares', 'Life's unfair', 'that's the way it is' ...)

Q What keeps happening to you? And what belief have you formed about this? (e.g. 'I never get promoted', 'No one values me', 'I'm always cheated on', I've never meet anyone who loves me'...)

YOUR EARLIEST JOB EXPERIENCES DIDN'T DEVELOP YOU

There are all sorts of reasons why you may not have had your dream start to a career. The biggest reason is likely to be one that's beyond your control, namely the economy. If you were embarking on your career during the recession, there were fewer opportunities available. You may have had a good start but then lost it as part of cut-backs. Taking a job just to earn some cash is all very well in the short term (for example as a student) because you know it's going to end. But when you feel stuck in a job and you're not developing your skills or yourself in any way, your self-esteem can suffer and you can end up believing that this is it for you, this is all you're worth.

If you have the negative belief that an unfulfilling job is all you deserve because you're not good enough, it's hard to shift places. But when you are able to separate what's within your control and what's not, you can then find ways to take charge of your life and develop yourself outside an unfulfilling job.

PROFESSOR FORTLOUIS WOOD ON HOW THE WORKPLACE CULTURE CAN DAMAGE REAL AMBITION

'The workplace system wants you to follow a known path and repeat or work within a narrow boundary. There isn't scope for reflective thought – to try things out, see how you feel, discover what you learn – to experiment. Yet reflection and analysis are essential in career development as well as problem-solving.

Unfortunately the culture in the workplace rewards people for marketing themselves rather than finding the best in themselves, something that can lead to premature career selection and narrowing of options. The economic downturn has made matters worse, with lean management strategies making everyone fight for their jobs, often working excessive hours and covering several jobs simultaneously. Some individuals report working 70 hours a week just to keep up. So ambition has been distorted and is more about sacrificing one's own needs (especially time to recharge and develop relationships) just to keep a job. Ambition, in a sense, is controlled by corporate structure and job codes or categories. People, particularly in large corporations, are moved around like widgets, treated as though they are interchangeable parts with coded identities. It's a brutal system where relationships and trust within work groups may be considered expendable in service of greater efficiency or flexibility. This isn't true everywhere or at all levels of any given company, but it's a prevalent model that is very oppressive and makes it difficult for individuals to find inspiration and opportunities for growth at work.'

ASK YOURSELF

Q What belief did you form about yourself in your first job?

Q How did your earliest work experiences make you feel about yourself?

Q To what extent does your job encourage you to be your authentic self?

Q My job makes me feel I am ... because every day I ...?

ARE YOU FRIGHTENED?

Yes, that small word 'fear' could be a big thing standing between you and success. However, it's only a major block if you think that absence of fear is a necessary ingredient. Even stage performers who are described as fearless will experience the symptoms of fear because these are normal hormonal changes. Actors are trained to handle these symptoms.

You might realize that your fear is way bigger than being nervous about isolated instances. We'll agree with you on this point. The bigger your dreams the bigger your fear, yes. But we're going to encourage and show you that you can substitute thrill for fear. When you go to a fairground and fear going up high and spinning round at great speed, you also know that's part of the thrill of the experience.

EXPERIENCE WITHOUT EXPECTATIONS

Mindfulness has become quite a buzzword, but it needn't be complicated or involve doing a course if for the moment you're not sure or simply don't have time. Something as simple as having a cup of tea and focusing your attention on the experience of drinking the tea can train your mind towards finding the ambitions that match your inner desires. 'As adults we build up fear and judgement and then inhibit our ability to have a true experience without expectation,' explains mind-body-movement coach Kele Baker. 'This is what mindfulness teaches us: not to have expectations. Have a raw, new experience instead.' So take a sip of tea, notice the temperature, then the taste; don't compare it to a previous experience of drinking tea.

We're not going to underestimate the emotional investment in change and how scary that is. That's why we advocate taking things step by step, and taking a holistic view of ambition. By looking at different areas of your life you can create support so that the major leaps you need to take become less scary.

In Chapter 4 we saw that successful people don't see screwing up as failure. You may have experienced failure, but you will have learnt something – if not a lot – about yourself. We also saw in Chapter 4 that grit is a key characteristic for success – and failure leads to grit. Not trying, not going for your dreams, not risking failure, not finding courage all amounts to staying in limbo, miserable and making do with a substandard life. And that's what is truly scary.

CHRIS BARÉZ-BROWN ON DEALING WITH FEAR

'We're all scared. The thing is, we're all cave men and our brain is scared of something new because this might eat us, so we see new things and think: danger, fear. We do things the way we've always done them – that's our reptilian brain. But we don't need to run away. To deal with what's going on in our brain we need to understand that this is happening. With this understanding, instead of reacting in our usual unconscious way (by running away from what we fear, or avoiding change), the key is to become conscious and ask: What's going on? Then we can choose to respond.

Fear and excitement feel the same in the body. That's the way you interpret and work with the feeling.

If you look at a negative reaction in an emotional way, you'll end up believing it and this belief will drive you: I'm scared, I'm not good enough, I'll fail. Instead you want to search for your healthy drivers: I want to make a difference, I want to entertain, I want to look after people.'

REAL PEOPLE

"Therapy helped me change how I think about myself." – James

'My parents said I had to make something of myself and without a degree I'd end up doing rubbish jobs. My dad made us go to a top school which I hated. I fell into being a rebel, making people laugh, smuggling in alcohol. I scraped through exams and made it into university. When I graduated I ended up in rubbish jobs, with debt from uni, and feeling bitter. After about three years things weren't any better.

Meanwhile my friends all seemed excited about their jobs, they were all getting laid or in love, and no girl was interested in me because I was a loser. I was drinking too much and doing drugs. I managed to get a job and started seeing someone, only she dumped me when I stormed out of the job because I hated it.

And then I crashed. My brother found me sobbing like a baby in the local park. I had a breakdown which made me feel ashamed. I saw a couple of therapists and hated therapy, but thanks to my brother I persevered and tried a third one who has been brilliant at helping me change how I think about myself.

I realized I had such a negative view of myself as well as a tendency to blame everybody and everything else around me rather than take any responsibility. Having an unbiased stranger really listen to me made such a difference.

I finally found the guts to start a stand-up comedy class after years of just talking about it. Instead of sitting around doing nothing and getting more depressed I accepted I had to do something, so I started working at a local pub for money. I was really chuffed that the owners and the manager asked me help them out in the business with my IT skills. I realized my university degree in IT wasn't as useless as I thought. Now I do their social media and blog too. I've also made friends with everyone working at the pub. They're all musicians, artists, writers, really cool people. I've changed a lot of my attitudes, namely that people working in bars must be students or losers. I'm even dating someone and feeling better about myself.

I still have issues with my dad which is hard, but now I understand that he just thought he was doing the right thing spending a fortune on my education because he didn't have this himself. When I told him I thought success to him was saying his sons were at a top school, he burst into tears. All he wanted was for us to have the head start he didn't have. Seeing my bossy controlling dad vulnerable has really helped. I want him to be proud of me.'

ASK YOURSELF

Q Every time something doesn't go right I always feel ... ?

Q What scares me most about making changes in my life is that ... ?

Q The last time I took a risk was ... and ... ?

Q The smallest step I can take to overcoming my fear about ... is to ... ?

We've given you a lot to reflect on in this chapter, from your childhood to your employment to date, from attitudes you may have unknowingly formed at school, to beliefs about the way you are that have become so entrenched in your mind you don't question them. Identifying what's in the way of your success can be a difficult process and we believe that you must treat yourself compassionately. In advocating a new model of ambition and success that isn't based on being ruthless, this means equally not being ruthless with yourself. That leads only to misery and unhappiness.

Instead of feeling bitter and falling into the trap of blaming people and situations, you can now work on making your mark as an individual. It's certainly never too late. One of the plusses of our society is that people can change careers, get married, have children, go round the world, campaign to save the world at any stage in their lives.

HOW DO YOU SABOTAGE YOURSELF?

What traps are you most likely to fall into?

Ever been called your own worst enemy? Sometimes, the only thing standing in the way of success is you. Is there always a reason why you don't go for that promotion or say yes to that opportunity to take your career in a new direction? If your friends are weary of hearing you moan about your lack of success, chances are you're putting obstacles in the way of your ambition. Change can be frightening, and however much we may want it, sometimes we can subconsciously act in a way that maintains the status quo, keeping us securely inside our comfort zone. But the first step to overcoming self-made barriers is to identify them. Take our quiz to find out which common self-sabotage habit you're most at risk of.

Test by Sally Brown

QUESTION 1

You bump into a friend you haven't seen for a while. How do you go about updating them on your life?

A. You tell them how nice it is to see them but you can't really talk now as you're running late.

B. You tell them about something that's gone well and that you're excited about, but can't help adding why you think you've not done as well as you should have.

C. You tell them a story about your latest disaster or problem at home or work.

D. You tell them how great it is you've bumped into them because you really need their help with your latest event/project.

QUESTION 2

Your boss gives you some urgent work to take home, due in first thing tomorrow, when you had planned to go out for dinner with friends. You:

A. Feel bad about cancelling dinner so end up staying up late to finish the work.

B. Fully intend to do it, but when you get home you realize you've left the work on your desk.

C. Beg a colleague who doesn't have much of a social life to do it for you.

D. Cancel the dinner, spend all evening on it but still worry that you haven't spent enough time on it.

QUESTION 3

Which statement best sums up your attitude to delegating?

A. I find most people are happy to help me out.

B. Most of the time it's just easier to do it myself.

C. Whenever I ask anyone to help, they end up letting me down.

D. I wonder if the other person will do it better than me.

QUESTION 4

You and a friend are running a marathon together. At the last minute, they pull out because of an injury. Do you:

A. Pull out as well, but tell everyone how much you wanted to do it.

B. Still do it, but feel so angry at your friend that you stop talking to them.

C. Feel too scared to do it alone, so get someone to do it with you.

D. Feel secretly relieved at the chance to pull out as you didn't really have time to do it in the first place.

QUESTION 5

What's your first thought when a colleague you don't know very well asks you to a dinner party?

A. Who else is going and is it worth my while?

B. I'd love to, but will I have enough to say?

C. Who has time for dinner parties?

D. Someone else must have dropped out.

QUESTION 6

Which statement best reflects your thoughts on luck?

A. Hard work is more reliable than good luck.

B. You make your own luck in life.

C. I seem to have more than my fair share of bad luck.

D. I don't like to tempt fate by dwelling on my good luck.

QUESTION 7

What was the best way of getting attention from your parents when you were growing up?

A. By being me – I was always centre of attention.

B. By getting top marks.

C. By being good and helping out.

D. By falling over or hurting myself.

QUESTION 8

What do you find the most surprising about your life as it is now?

A. That I've got as far as I have.
B. That I manage to keep going.
C. That I'm not more successful.
D. That so much keeps going wrong.

Now, add up your scores from each answer using the following table, and find out how you sabotage yourself:

	A	B	C	D
Q1	3	2	1	4
Q2	3	1	4	2
Q3	4	3	1	2
Q4	1	4	2	3
Q5	4	2	3	1
Q6	3	4	1	2
Q7	4	2	3	1
Q8	2	3	4	1

If you scored between 8 and 13 ...

Watch out for poor-me syndrome

There's always a reason why things haven't turned out the way you want them to, whether it's that someone has let you down, or it's simply been bad luck. But the truth is, your mind latches onto problems like a heat-seeking missile. However much you may talk about making a change that will further your ambition, you can also come up with a long list of very plausible sounding reasons why it can't happen right now. A part of you is suspicious of success – what if you get what you want and it doesn't make you happy? Or it means people don't like you anymore? By putting barriers in the way of your success, you can stay inside your comfort zone. But there's a part of you that *does* want more, or you wouldn't have picked up this book in the first place. Next time you feel yourself giving up at the first hurdle, ask yourself if there's a way round this challenge, then pick yourself up and keep going. You are stronger than you think – it's time to get into the driving seat of your life and put your foot down on the pedal!

If you scored between 14 and 20 ...

Watch out for imposter syndrome

You're holding on to a belief that success is something that happens to other people, not you, and you've only got as far as you have by sheer luck. You've set yourself an invisible bar which limits you to achieving a certain level of success. Your perfectionist tendencies may hold you back from applying for promotions or jobs unless you feel you 100% meet all the criteria. You've also got a very vivid imagination that can conjure all the possible pitfalls of stepping out of your comfort zone and challenging yourself. The upside of constantly doubting your abilities means you'll never rest on your laurels and always put in extra effort, but in the long term, imposter syndrome can generate anxiety and undermine your mental wellbeing. When you find yourself doubting your ability, use a CBT technique – ask yourself: 'Is this really the case? What evidence is there?' It may also help to compile physical evidence of your success (e.g. by creating a folder on your PC where you keep complimentary emails or pieces of work you're proud of) to help counteract that doubting voice in your head.

If you scored between 21 and 27 ...

Watch out for busy syndrome

You were brought up to think hard work is the way to success, and there's a lot of truth in that. But what's just as important is working smart, making sure your time, energy and headspace is spent on the right things. When you're conscientious and capable at work, you can become the person who is always landed with last-minute projects, especially if those above you know that you'll say yes to extra work and get on with it without making a fuss. You may also have fallen into the trap of equating a busy life with a successful one. But being too busy can ultimately sabotage your ambition, and put you at risk of burnout. What can you say no to, to free up more time for the things that really matter?

If you scored between 28 and 32 ...

Watch out for superstar syndrome

You're a proactive person with lots of ideas, enthusiasm and motivation, and you've never been plagued by low self-esteem, but at times your ego can over-inflate, sabotaging your ambition. Have you ever turned down a chance to take your career in a new direction because it would mean taking a temporary drop in wages or loss of a status job title? You may also have quite rigid ideas of how people should treat you, taking offence where none is intended, and at times placing overly high expectations on people. Your biggest barrier to success is a sense of entitlement, and it's worth reminding yourself that no successful person got where they are today without hard work and determination.

CHAPTER 6

AMBITION TRAPS

As we discussed in Chapter 1, ambition has come to be associated with hardness: being hard in the ruthless sense and being hard to achieve. You know by this point that we're coming at ambition from a different route and we're stripping it of all the negative associations. Why would striving for something better or something amazing be a bad thing? In this chapter we want to flag up the traps that you can easily and unwittingly fall into. These are the traps that can lead you back to old-style ambition and away from real ambition. Climbing out of these traps is difficult to impossible, all the more so because they are pretty much invisible.

Ambition traps prevent you from knowing who you are so that you find your real ambitions. Our aim so far has been to show you that matching your inner to your outer ambitions is the key. If you would love to feel accomplished plus you love studying, for example, then studying to a PhD level might match this inner desire and inner passion. If you would love to feel accomplished but loath studying, then accomplishing a practical challenge would be the way to go.

Of course, questioning yourself, brainstorming with yourself, assessing and reviewing yourself takes time. We want to help you remove anything that makes the process hard. We want you to see this as a fascinating process rather than a difficult one. We don't want you sidetracked by any traps.

As we enter adulthood, we enter various worlds where things are set. You may be working for a corporate environment where sales goals are the mark of success; all your friends might have a set view of relationships being about marriage (or not). The days, weeks, months, even years go by, and you know you are dissatisfied and bored to the point of not knowing what it is you want. However, you might not be aware of what's robbing you of your ability to desire something new and your belief that achieving this is possible.

Of our 10 ambition traps, some or most may apply to you to varying degrees. To help you analyse yourself further we have some additional Ask Yourself questions at the end of each trap to help you identify your personal traps. Awareness in itself will help to fuel rather than drain your ambition. After reading this chapter, you will sense your mind lighting up when it recognizes a trap and you can steer clear.

1. EGO-BASED AMBITION

In Chapter 2 we got to the bottom of what you want. This hopefully means you now know that your unmet needs can be driving what you (think you) want. In Chapter 3 we introduced the concept of values, and living your life according to your values – what's important to you and what ignites your spirit. Your ego can get in the way of both your unmet needs and values.

There are two ways ego-based ambition manifests itself. One way is when your mind tricks you into believing that you have to refuse an opportunity because it's not good enough for you. You're better than the opportunity. Let's say you change careers and qualify in a new skill – but don't want to start at the bottom all over again in your new career because you 'deserve' something better. Here's where you need to take an honest look at yourself to see if you're genuinely underselling yourself, or letting go of an opportunity for experience. The two are very different. Sometimes it's impossible to be objective, so it makes sense to seek guidance from a coach, a mentor or a good friend who is experienced in this field.

> **"When you focus on ego and wanting prestige you can miss out because you're not looking at all the options available to you."**
>
> Kele Baker, mind-body-movement coach

The second way your ego can be a trap is by getting in the way of what you love by tricking you into believing that there's only one way. Let's say you hate your job and deep down want to be a travel writer. But your belief is that it's impossible to make a living as a travel writer. Here's where you need to go back and get clear about your unmet needs and your values. If your unmet need is independence, what else can you do to feel you're independent and not controlled? If your values are freedom, travel and exploration, what else other than or in addition to travel writing can you do to meet these values?

When you put your ego aside, you can research to find different routes to your dreams. How are other people living their dream, what lessons can you learn from them?

> 66 **People often start out in one area of a career and discover a whole world that ultimately leads them to their calling.** 99
>
> Lisa Fortlouis Wood, Professor of Psychology and licensed clinical psychologist

So long as you're not being exploited, an opportunity to do something in an area you love is better than no opportunity. Allowing your ego to trick you into believing that you deserve nothing less than the most prestigious position is far from self-esteem. As Professor of Psychology and licensed clinical psychologist Lisa Fortlouis Wood puts it, 'only wanting the top spot is all or nothing thinking'.

ASK YOURSELF

 I know it's my ego's voice when I tell myself that ...?

 What have you said no to recently? In which of these cases was your ego behind the no?

 A different way of doing what I love might be ... ?

2. OBSESSION WITH FAME

This ambition trap often goes hand in hand with the ego-based trap, especially in ambitions connected to entertainment and the arts, politics and business. In Chapter 2 we saw that fame is not one of the basic human needs for happiness. Psychologists have not established that fame equates with fulfilment. In this chapter we want to go deeper and clarify how one might not even be aware that this is an obsession that is a block.

Sometimes the obsession with fame masks a fear of failure. Are you not finishing that novel because you're genuinely developing your writing skills and giving it your best shot – or because finishing means having to send it out and risk rejection? Are you fantasizing about being on the bestseller list or top of the music charts or head of a global business empire but you're not *doing* anything about it?

This is where you need to know deep down to your core whether you are passionate about music/art/dance/books/film/business/politics or you're passionate about being a star. The problem with being focused on stardom is that it's one of those things that you can't control. It's dependent on so many other factors and other people.

An obsession with fame is all around us. This means people around you might be making undermining comments about competitive fields they know nothing about. In other words, they are affected by the celebrity culture and consider themselves experts. If you want to write, sing, act, lead, innovate and you announce this to all and sundry then all sorts of people will be making flip comments like: Oh, have you got a book deal yet? Are you going on X Factor? Are you going to Hollywood? Will you go on Dragon's Den? Will you join a political party? Even if you want to start a blog you'll have people saying: Oh, so will you be famous like that Deliciously Ella?

If everybody around you seems fame obsessed, you risk falling into a negative mindset that unless you achieve fame your pursuit is meaningless. The problem is that once you're in that cycle of thinking, fame is least likely to happen. Remember that people who have achieved tremendous fame and success, from Madonna to Jeff Bezos, have primarily been obsessed with being their super-selves.

ASK YOURSELF

Q If I was famous it would mean I am ... ?

Q Fame to me means ... ?

Q I would rather be ... and ... than famous

3. WORKING TOO HARD

Of course you need to apply yourself to doing something little by little to achieve what you want. And yes, of course you have to work (hard) at it. However, this doesn't mean exhausting yourself.

As we saw in Chapter 1, old ambition came to mean overdoing one ambition, usually work, but real ambition is balance and nurturing. One major study[1] in 2012 found that working long hours is correlated with an increased likelihood of depression.

Working *too* hard can be one of the traps masking a victim attitude and unmet needs: 'look at me, no one works harder than me, I can't do anything more, there must be something wrong with me, life is so unfair …' If you're working too hard you need to be honest with yourself and probe at the unmet needs underlying this.

> **" If you are struggling then you have to ask yourself why. Effort is a good thing – but it's not the only ingredient. "**
>
> John Purkiss, headhunter and coach

If you feel that making an effort in any area in your life is a struggle that isn't yielding results then you need to reevaluate the effort. Whether it's going online to line up dates every day so you can find love, or working evenings and weekends so you can be promoted, if you're exhausted from working too hard at it then you need to change this. Purkiss suggests looking and learning from other people: 'It's instructive to look sideways at what others are doing that is working.'

One of the reasons people fall into the trap of working too hard is because success has been associated with reaching the top of a work pyramid where people earn the most and have the most prestigious title. But if, as coach John Purkiss suggests, you take a sideways look at life, you can channel energy elsewhere.

PROFESSOR FORTLOUIS WOOD ON HOW MENTORSHIP CAN HELP YOU

- *'Effective and sensitive mentoring can be extremely useful even if you know your path.*

- *Direct feedback from mentors can help you become clearer in prioritizing goals and selecting the best training experiences.*

- *It's possible to balance independence with sensitive guidance and advice, particularly if you are in a competitive workplace, in graduate school or making a life transition.*

- *A person who has experience and information and who listens well can support you in developing a plan that fits your interests and circumstances. This person is an important ally in helping you make the best decisions.'*

ASK YOURSELF

Q If I stopped working so hard, what would happen is ...

Q If I worked a little less/tried a bit less, what would happen is ...

Q What do your answers reveal about how you view yourself?

Q If I had more time I would ...

Q The one area in my life where no matter how hard I try nothing happens is ...

4. THE PRESSURE TO FIT IN

Are you in an environment where the pressure to fit in drains your energy, your creativity and your individuality? You feel so stifled by what's around you that you even believe it's your fault. You may be tormenting yourself as to why you can't fit in and doing your best to somehow go along with what's around you. Whether you're dressing in a way that makes you feel boxed and boring, or putting yourself through social events that make your heart sink, you're likely to feel like a bird resigned to being caged. An awareness of feeling caged will at least set your wings flapping to get out. A resignation to fitting in dampens your inner spirit.

We know from behavioural scientists that the pressure to conform is natural in human beings. That's why wanting to break out of the norm feels deeply uncomfortable. Groundbreaking research[2] in 2009 led by Dr Vasily Klucharev from the F.C. Donders Center for Cognitive Neuroimaging in the Netherlands found that the brain is programmed to conform. Neurons in the brain detect non-conformity and send an error signal. In other words we're programmed to go along with the norm.

You may not even know you feel pressure to fit in. Some clues are: you've always got niggly illnesses, you know you're drinking too much to feel better, or you have to drink when you're out doing what your friends always want to do, you feel apathetic at weekends, you hate Sunday evenings because it's back to the box on Monday, you feel drained when you're surrounded by people, you constantly want to retreat on your own.

Being aware of the pressure to fit in can help you find strategies (perhaps through a mentor or coach) to deal with the situation(s). You might be able to change the environment (e.g. changing jobs), or you might seek out different social situations where you are able to show who you are (e.g. through taking a course with like-minded people).

If you're in an environment where you have to conform, yet your desire is to be promoted and shake things up, then you can look for small ways in which to be you – even it's just wearing mis-matched socks or a colour that becomes you. If it's your friends you have to fit in with, remember it's a big wide world with new friendship webs to discover.

ASK YOURSELF

Q To fit in at work I have to ...

Q What my friends don't know about me is that ...

Q I wish with my family I could be ...

Q I want to live somewhere where everyone is ...

5. EXPECTING PERFECTION

When you are looking at all the areas of your life, it's natural to desire the best for yourself. Why wouldn't you want a lovely home, love and romance, loving friends and family, and a great lifestyle? Well that's a bit of a catch question. If your framework for everything is a perfect and abstract lovely, it's going to be unattainable. Perfection doesn't exist. It's a fantasy. Even high achievers who have created what you may consider a perfect life have imperfect aspects in their lives. One 2012 study in Canada[3] found that perfectionists suffered health problems as a result of the stress from setting themselves high standards.

It's useful here to refer to other ways of viewing life, like Chinese philosophy. You've no doubt seen the yin and yang, black and white symbol. Mind-body-movement coach Kele Baker explains that the reason there is no rigid line between the two, and there is a white dot in the black area and vice versa, is because this symbolizes that there's always an interplay between the two energies. And this applies to all areas of our life.

If you expect that a city, a home, a job, a relationship will be perfect, then you are setting yourself unrealistic goals and lining yourself up with disappointment. Baker explains that it's figuring the balance that's important. Are you *more* satisfied (by a city, home, job, relationship, hobby etc.) or *less* satisfied? What's the balance?

❝ Life isn't black or white. Nothing in our lives is ever just one thing. ❞

Kele Baker, mind-body-movement coach

ASK YOURSELF

Q Identify the main areas in your life. What's the balance between you being happy/unhappy in these areas?

Q What are you regularly complaining about? Create a checklist of the negatives as well as the positives. What's the balance? Can you re-evaluate how you feel?

6. QUITTING TOO EARLY

This is related to high and unrealistic expectations, but in this case the expectations are about you and your abilities, and how you perceive you 'should' be doing and what you 'should' have achieved. If you place unrealistic expectations on yourself, then you won't give yourself the time you need for your journey.

> 66 **Constantly evaluating yourself with the expectation that you should be better can lead to giving up, especially early on.** 99

Lisa Fortlouis Wood, Professor of Psychology and licensed clinical psychologist

At this point you might find these references to roads and journeys irritating. You may have formed the opinion that if it's meant to be, if you're truly meant to do whatever, if you're talented, and if you visualize the success, and 'it' still hasn't happened, then you might as well give up. Remember in Chapter 5, when we looked at why some people achieve their ambitions, one of the reasons we highlighted was grit. Quitting too early doesn't help you develop grit. It reinforces in some part of your mind a sense of failure.

When your driving instructor nags you to check your mirror for what's going on behind you, would you quit learning to drive? Of course not. Yet you might be quitting your ambition(s) because of an equally 'silly' reason. If you were to announce that online dating is a total waste of time and that's it, there's no one out there for you anyway, and somebody who loves you pointed out that you have to be proactive with online dating (and showed you how), would you really quit your desire to love and be loved? Wouldn't you have just another go to see what happens?

If you are setting yourself rigid goals you might inadvertently be setting yourself up to quit early. To avoid this, do your research. Your ambition is to write thrillers? How long did it take your favourite bestselling thriller writers to get to the bestselling spots – and how did they get there? Terry Hayes,[4] was a journalist and scriptwriter before he wrote international bestseller *I am Pilgrim*. Gillian Flynn[5] was a journalist and TV critic before she wrote thrillers, and it was her third, *Gone Girl*, that became an international sensation. And Paula Hawkins[6] was a financial journalist who wrote four romantic fiction novels under a pseudonym before the thriller that made her name globally: *Girl on the Train*.

In business there are similar stories.[7] Sony, co-founded by Akio Morita, might be a fave TV brand now, but one its first products was an inefficient rice cooker. Before turning Windows into a world-brand synonymous with computers, Bill Gates had a company called Traf-o-Data that didn't go very far. Colonel Sanders founded KFC at the age of 65, after over 1,000 rejections for his fried chicken.

Whatever your heart is set on doing, let your heart (rather than a constructed chart of 'should') guide you.

ASK YOURSELF

 Which area in your life – however small – have you given up on too early? Think of any hobbies, careers, passions, gym memberships, healthy eating regimes you have abandoned quickly. What were the reasons?

7. EXTERNAL AMBITION

If you don't do the soul-searching that we recommend to find out what really makes you tick, the danger is that you base your aspirations only on what can be seen: money, material items, job titles, praise or prizes. Of course it's natural to want a secure job when you've been unemployed, a debt-free partner if you had to carry a previous partner financially; and there's nothing wrong with aspiring to owning fast cars and designer clothes. It's just that if this is all your ambition is based on, there isn't enough inner fuel to drive you to success. There's a difference between 'I really want to create a business because no one else has thought of my idea; when I make it yippee, I can buy myself a sports car', and 'I want to run a business that makes me the money I want to buy a sports car'.

The danger with externally based ambition is that it can lead you to making choices that don't benefit all areas of your life. Through externally based ambition you can end up adding previous traps to the equation: working too hard, expecting perfection, being driven by ego and making decisions based on prestige.

A 2014 study at the University of California, Berkeley,[8] revealed that a preoccupation with wealth and status went hand-in-hand with mental disorders including depression and aggression. What's interesting about this particular study is that whether people achieved the status or didn't, the effect was similar.

> **❝ If everything about your ambition is based on external motivations, then it's likely to be false or short-lived. ❞**
>
> Lisa Fortlouis Wood, Professor of Psychology and licensed clinical psychologist

External ambition can be like wearing somebody else's mask. Not only is it ambition that might be masking somebody else's insecurities, you're now trying to make the mask fit you. It'll be wonky and uncomfortable at best – and constricting at worst. Remember that real ambition comes from within.

ASK YOURSELF

 Where did your ideas of success come from?

 Do your external ambitions match your true internal desires? (If you're not sure, give yourself time to brainstorm and think further about your internal desires.)

8. IMITATION AMBITION

One of the dangers of growing up with, and watching too much of, reality TV, along with the huge celebrity culture around us, is the desire to imitate lifestyles. The celebrity/reality TV culture extends from TV to social media so you might also be following Vloggers and Instagrammers who appear to have enviable and easy lifestyles you want to imitate.

As Professor Fortlouis Wood puts it, our society is losing its sense of the work ethic. To spell out what we mean by work ethic, it's about exploring what you want, working towards it, and achieving your goals. That's not boring is it? Yet a culture has evolved that has you believe that you could live just like these stars.

We're not saying don't be inspired, we're saying have a little word with yourself. How much of what you do comes from you, and how much is imitation? Are you eating avocado because it's an Instagram sensation or because you love it, it's good as part of a healthy filling lunch, and you've found where to buy nice ripe ones? Start to check in on the details that make your life. Make it a habit to check in and ask yourself why you want what you want. Do you want that Michael Kors bag in another colour because your colleagues will be impressed? Do you want that iPhone watch because women you're dating will be impressed?

" When people watch too much TV, and TV provides the basis for their social identities, they are more likely to come across to themselves and others as fake. "

Lisa Fortlouis Wood, Professor of Psychology and licensed clinical psychologist

Allowing imitation ambition to take over all areas of your life has a cumulative effect: it erodes your ability to find your calling and follow your heart. Imitation ambition can be a more lethal trap than external ambition. If you're fired up to achieve externally, you're fired up for something. Imitation ambition is deceptive – it has you believe you don't have to do much.

ASK YOURSELF

Q Where do your ideas of success come from? Can you name them?

Q List the last 10 items you bought – and write down what precisely made you buy these. Is there a pattern?

Q My ideas of what I want originate from ...

9. SOCIAL MEDIA

We can't avoid social media as not only is it a part of our lives, it's also essential for many aspects of creating success. From setting up a business to self-publishing a book, you need to master social media to market your business and yourself. Consider it a little like alcohol. One drink too many and you can go from merry to martyr. The thing is with alcohol, when it comes down to it people know what the risks are, whether they're overdoing it, how much their bodies can take. With social media, however, there are no guidelines or government health warnings.

PROFESSOR FORTLOUIS WOOD ON THE DEBILITATING SIDE OF SOCIAL MEDIA

'What I see in my clinical practice is that young adults who are insecure about where they are in their life and development look at other people's social media pages and feel terrible about how they are doing. They see themselves as losing out or failing – even when they are making progress in finding their path, making friends and learning about relationships. This can be debilitating. Then there is the other side of the problem when people present themselves as having a much better time than they really are. This can happen when people don't really share how hard it is to manage the challenges and stress at work, or in relationships, or in parenting. They don't talk enough about the reality of the day-to-day and ups and downs. This can be hard for some to decipher and can lead to discouragement and competition that isn't productive.

Although social media can be beneficial and can lead to very useful support from friends who are far away, it isn't necessarily a safe place to share the details of one's life or work. Another danger of spending too much time on

Facebook and other sites is that you are not focusing on your own experiences and what is meaningful and working well for you. Just having your own experiences without sharing and getting feedback is important for developing independence and a sense of grounding.

So, for many people, Facebook provides a sense of belonging that makes them feel part of something larger – whether an intimate group, a political or social community, or the wider world. But one probably can't get a true sense of belonging solely through Facebook. If we don't have people close to us, and all we have is social media, there can be a sense of isolation and alienation, especially for those who are in a vulnerable place. That is where finding help and support comes in.'

OVERCOME YOUR FEAR OF SOCIAL MEDIA – AND USE IT AS A TOOL FOR SUCCESS

Whether social media-shy or lacking the technology skills, there's no escaping social media as a tool for success. It's a skill one has to learn just like any other. Baker advises that instead of allowing your mind to get overwhelmed with fear and doing nothing, you start with what might be essential right now, and what you can handle: 'Start by slowly building an inner sense of comfort handling the technology, then slowly build on confidence.' Tackling the technology and how you feel step by step will help you find what suits you and works for you.

10. LIVING FOR THE WEEKEND

We've mentioned working too hard, but the opposite of that is not working at all to pursue your dreams. If you are also so bored that you live for the weekend when you can party, watch sport for hours, do nothing, then you'll have slipped into one of the biggest traps.

> 66 **Not pursuing your own creativity will eventually leave you stagnant and frustrated.** 99

Lisa Fortlouis Wood, Professor of Psychology and licensed clinical psychologist

It's most likely that if you are in this situation, it's the easy thing to do. You might even be a little proud of the fact that your partying friends love you so much they don't want you to miss out, or it's so awful living at home with your parents you absolutely have to get out a lot at weekends. Either scenario is a big trap that you set yourself. With no real reason to kick you into making a jump into the unknown you can carry on with the safety offered by instant and guaranteed gratification.

Here's where if you didn't have the means to go out partying you might develop the impulse for ambition. Immigrants tend to be ambitious because they leave behind a life that isn't easy. That decision to leave their country requires courage, but once they take that decision the motivation to create a new life follows. They build on small successes, are grateful for opportunities in their new country, but most of all develop an ambition muscle. It's the same, Professor Fortlouis Wood explains, for people who leave home early because home wasn't an easy or happy place. 'When they see that they can make it on their own, they become more ambitious.'

If having a good time at weekends is the easy way out, think about creating some discomfort for yourself by facing up to how you really feel and looking for ways to live every day rather than just the weekend.

STOP MOANING

Instead of moaning, reflect on the situation and your relationship to it. Are you moaning about the weather because you can't think of anything else to say to colleagues or neighbours? Can you find a different way to make small talk about the weather?

When you stop moaning it boosts your ability to get on with changing whatever causes you to moan, or finding ways to adapt. Chris Baréz-Brown warns that moaning is more than an addictive habit. 'Moaning is a way of stating that there's nothing wrong with you, it's whatever you're moaning about that's the problem. Moaning deflects from the fact that you're not happy about who you are.'

In this chapter we've confronted you with some personal truths that might even have made you feel uncomfortable. We'd have liked to have given you a list of zany ambition traps that would make you feel 'oh right, avoid Know-it-all-Nigel and Me-me-me-Emily'. These ambition traps aren't so clear-cut that they can be instantly avoided because mostly they come from within.

Spend some time on really thinking about the questions raised in this chapter. You might even consider discussing them with friends. You might be surprised to discover that your friends feel similarly to you but feel they have to put up a front when you're all out at weekends. You might feel like an alien realizing that everyone around you is more interested in accumulating things – which could lead you to finding fellow aliens and forming a tribe.

Figuring out the negative stuff in our heads is not a negative process. It's like doing a proper clean up and tidy when your home's got into a bit of a mess. You can give that pan you use for a stir-fry a good scrub – or ditch it and buy a shiny one. A new shiny pan might be what you need to actually cook more, and that includes more dishes than stir-fry.

As you identify what erodes your real ambition, you'll have many 'aha' moments. These 'aha' moments will light you up and empower you to learn how to be successful.

ASK YOURSELF

Q How much of a good time do you have at weekends?

Q Do you say no to going out so that you can spend time on developing your dream?

Q The time I devote to making my dreams happen at the weekend is ...

Q My social life gets in the way of me ...

Q I fritter my time with ... and then I feel ...

Q My biggest fear about not seeing my mates as much so that I can work on my ambitions is ...

Q If I'm really honest about what I do at the weekend I feel ...

Q My biggest trap is ... because ...

Q I need to learn to ... so that I don't get tempted or swayed by ...

3 HOW CAN YOU ACHIEVE YOUR AMBITIONS?

CHAPTER 7

CAN YOU LEARN TO BE AMBITIOUS?

T
he question we ask isn't 'is there a magic formula for ambition?' but 'can you learn to be ambitious?' Wanting to learn how to fuel your ambition for the best life you can create for yourself (and how to nurture the individual ambitions within this stable) means you will be opening yourself up to all sorts of possibilities. Your willingness to learn shows an understanding that things will happen stage by stage, step by step. Provided you accept that learning is a process that requires effort and patience and the results are incremental, you won't be disappointed.

We hope by now that you believe it's possible to *try* and learn something that can lead to success for you. This belief in itself is a huge advantage. As we saw in Chapter 4, a growth mindset rather than a fixed mindset is one of the main reasons behind success. You may not have achieved your dreams to date, but it may simply not be your time yet. As we saw in Chapter 6, quitting too early is an ambition trap.

66 If you learn what motivates you, then you can harness ambition. 99

Dannie-Lu Carr, creativity specialist, communications consultant & creative practitioner

Given that at the heart of real ambition is learning who you are inside – from knowing your needs to your values – by delving into yourself you are already learning to be ambitious. In this chapter you will discover how to take this learning process further. You can learn to be ambitious by understanding how your brain engages with your mind's desires and knowing the psychology of motivation. You can learn how to ignite your motivation to make things happen in your life.

PROFESSOR FORTLOUIS WOOD ON USING OUR EXPERIENCES TO ACCESS OUR POTENTIAL

'What I have learned over many years of studying psychology, is that people vary significantly in their desire for novelty, tolerance for ambiguity, persistence in the face of obstacles, need for control and independence, desire for contact with others, and need for approval and a sense of fitting in. My style of working, exploring, problem solving, creating and choosing is not right for everyone. The important key is to look at your patterns of behaviour and what works and doesn't work for you. These are important clues to what kind of experiences induce growth and allow you to fulfil your potential.

- Do you prefer working with others, or like helping others who have a vision to make that come to life?

- Do you like to go home after work and not have to think about it again until you return the next day?

- Do you prefer large projects? Or do you like smaller jobs that are completed in a brief time span?

- What other goals do you have and how will they fit with your work style?

These and other questions are important to answer. But it takes time and reflection on what is working and why. Here is where mentorship, advice and learning from experts can be especially helpful.'

UNDERSTANDING WILLPOWER

The great thing about understanding willpower is that it's one of the most researched areas in psychology. At the forefront of the research, with decades of clinical trials and highly regarded research analysis, is social psychologist Roy Baumeister. Baumeister's research, encapsulated in his book,[1] illustrates that willpower isn't finite. We don't have an endless supply available.

According to Baumeister,[2] everything we do in modern life uses up our willpower stock. Those normal everyday things, which could include a long convoluted commute to work, some challenges in work, and limited time to shop and cook, all use up your reserves. Then the more problems you add (like illness, divorce, redundancy), the more the stock becomes depleted. What's reassuring is that if you feel that you've been drained by several problems, you don't need to feel guilty about not having the will (power) to change things. Once you learn how willpower operates, what becomes apparent is that it's all about timing. If you learn to pace and time your ambitions, you are more likely to succeed.

Another key finding from Baumeister is that our brain does not distinguish between the energy we need to make a career change, and the energy we need to confront a difficult boss. Studies[3] even show that people with chronic pain have a shortage of willpower. The brain doesn't seem to be on our side when it comes to willpower because it doesn't edit.

Baumeister's studies have shown that we need willpower to control our thoughts, emotions and impulses. According to Baumeister one of the keys to harnessing willpower in order to make positive changes in life is to first identify the signs of depletion. Put a different way, by identifying what you feel is draining you in your life you can then work out whether you can eliminate this, or focus on dealing with the problems.

Making two major changes at once is challenging. Baumeister's advice is to start with the easier thing to change, get some practice and build up self-control. The good news is that willpower is like a muscle: exercise it regularly and it gets stronger. Learning to make small and simple changes in all areas of your life boosts and supports your ability to make one major change at a time.

RESIST SHOPPING WHEN YOU'RE DOWN

You have a bad day in what you feel is a dead-end job where you're not appreciated, so you go shopping and buy yourself something to cheer yourself up. Normal, right? Yes, but shopping is best avoided during negative circumstances. According to recent research,[4] shopping to boost self-esteem can in fact backfire. Shopping is a habit that affects self-control. After the 'high' it's a return to the low feelings and these can intensify.

THE SURPRISING FOUNDATION OF WILLPOWER

In 2012, we interviewed Baumeister[5] and one of the biggest impressions he made on us was his emphasis on how important it is to look after oneself by eating healthily, exercising, relaxing and sleeping. 'Exhaustion saps self-control,' he stressed.

One of the most surprising elements that boosts willpower is energy from food. The brain needs glucose because this is converted into neurotransmitters – the messengers to your brain. Studies[6] on people with low glycaemia show they have more trouble concentrating. Baumeister's mantra is: 'No glucose, No willpower.'[7] When our brain's glucose level is low it gets cranky.

That's when some parts go into a high gear, and other parts collapse. Unfortunately what goes into high gear is the part of the brain that craves sugar and alcohol. And what shuts down is the part of the brain responsible for ambition.

Something as simple as giving up dieting and focusing on learning to eat healthily instantly increases the willpower you need to become more ambitious. What Baumeister and his team of scientists have confirmed with their extensive studies is that wellbeing boosts willpower. Sure, there are plenty of 'successful' people who drink too much, don't sleep enough and don't eat healthily – but as we established in Part 1 this is old-style ambition that leads to burnout and health problems rather than balanced success.

> **"Fresh air gives us oxygen which we need to think creatively about what we want in life. And we need to keep moving to clear our heads and to generate more energy. "**
>
> Dannie-Lu Carr, creativity specialist, communications consultant & creative practitioner

YOUR BRAIN AND WILLPOWER

Another leading authority on willpower, health psychologist Kelly McGonigal[8] from Stanford University, explains that our brain is divided into three parts:

1. I will (would like to do more of)
2. I won't (must give up a habit)
3. I want (a long-term goal).

This is based on studies by neuroscientists who have identified the different parts of the brain. McGonigal's course 'The Science of Willpower'[9] is based on understanding this. Learning to be ambitious comes down to learning how your brain manages willpower.

It's important to remember that alcohol shuts down the 'I want' part of your brain. The 'I won't' part can dominate the trio if you let it, so if most of your thoughts are 'I won't' the other two give up because the brain is geared up to do the hardest thing it perceives it has to do.

Let's say you want to set up a business and be your own boss. This means you will have to learn how to do so, which might involve taking a course or doing some research, working out how to save money so that you have a financial cushion, figuring out whether you can start from home, and creating a plan for development. However, adding to this equation a strict diet in which your mind is preoccupied with I won't eat this I won't eat that, plus alcohol to comfort your frustration, and all your good work is undone.

When we interviewed McGonigal for the magazine[10] her advice was to reframe intentions by turning 'resistant thoughts' into positive goals. 'I will eat and drink healthily' helps your brain do the job of keeping your eating and drinking habits on track without upsetting your other goals.

Anything you can do to feel good wires up the brain for positive actions and long-term rewards. Going back to our balanced model of success, planning some time to yourself to pursue a hobby like hiking might seem an indulgence when you 'should' be focusing on what you're led to believe is a more serious aspect of success. But in fact, walking your way through more and more demanding routes trains your mind to take action towards a long-term goal. It's also training your mind to take action in other areas of your life too. Whether you're hiking, walking, dancing, baking, cooking – whatever the hobby, consider it your mind-gym.

If instead of following your urge to walk, bake or dance (or whatever hobby you are inclined to do) you resist the urge and procrastinate, in so doing you're further depleting your willpower. Baumeister's studies have confirmed that procrastination is the biggest enemy to willpower because your brain is caught up avoiding rather than doing.

A typical scenario, like putting off running after work with the excuse that staying behind will make you look keener and signify you deserve a promotion, really doesn't work. You're much more likely to impress your boss with your commitment to running – and the physical and mental energy you gain from running will feed back into your work anyway.

One of the biggest brain drains of course is technology, not just because it wastes time but because of how it insidiously affects our brain chemistry. When we interviewed McGonigal for the magazine she explained that technology is 'an instant hit of dopamine'. The problem is when the brain gets a hit of the pleasure-hormone dopamine, that instant hit sucks up the willpower reserves too. So rather than using technology to monitor what everyone else is doing on social media, put a time limit on that aspect, and use technology in the way that McGonigal advises: to research (towards your ambition) and to build a support network (for your ambition).

YOUR BRAIN AND GOALS

Learning how you personally respond to different goals is a big part of achieving your goals. Start by letting go of the idea that successful people are great at meeting *all* their goals.

One of the leading experts on goal setting is social psychologist Heidi Grant Halvorson.[11] In her revealing book *Succeed*[12] she recommends identifying *now* versus *later* goals and understanding how these work. Halvorson explains that these relate to *why* and *what* thinking. When we're thinking about why we want something this tends to be a future-based goal. When we're thinking about what we can do, these goals tend to be about something now or in the near future. The problem if you're only setting later goals is your brain might be getting excited by what you desire – but you're not propelled to take action. It's the now goals that kickstart your mind into identifying how to overcome obstacles.

To complicate matters, Halvorson goes on to explain the difference between a goal you want because it's going to make you feel/look good, or a goal that will make you better at doing something you want to do. The studies that she points to are unanimous in their conclusions: focusing on getting better at something is the way to go for achieving long-term goals because you're less likely to give up and because your focus is on the journey.[13] As Halvorson strongly advises, when you need persistence then you need to set get-better goals.[14]

PROFESSOR FORTLOUIS WOOD ON HOW TO FIND THE RIGHT GOALS

- *'Before setting any goals, find your motivational inspiration – what works for you.*
- *What did you love in school? What activities captured your interest? There will be clues here that will help you now.*
- *What do you do that makes you lose track of time? Is it making things? It is moving? Is it music?*
- *Have you envisioned yourself living or working away from your current environment? Do you feel you would fit in somewhere else or with other people? Where is that and with whom?*
- *Is there something you want for yourself, something perhaps that others don't want you to be or don't see as fitting who you are? It's important to have your own vision.'*

The key to learning to be ambitious is learning to harness the power of our brain. And, as we've seen in this chapter, thankfully there is plenty of science to inform us how the brain works. It's important not to forget this knowledge exists, particularly when something like a new dieting or health regime becomes fashionable. Anything that inflicts rules on your life distracts the brain. So at least you can chuckle now and chuck out the must-dos and must-bes in your life, along with the shoulds, whatever they are. These deplete your power to decide and act on what you will do.

Learning what inspires you and motivates you is the first step. The second is combining this with learning how to keep your willpower fully stocked through your wellbeing. This is a 'formula' we can give you because we know there is plenty of science behind it. You don't have to feel you're not one of those people who manage to be ambitious and successful. By looking after yourself and knowing yourself, success on your terms will follow.

THINK OF YOUR GOALS AS SMALL STEPS TO YOUR DREAM

When setting goals, it's tempting to think big, but in fact you need to think in terms of small steps toward achieving your dreams. Dannie-Lu Carr advises creating a 3–5 year rough plan, and within this plan outlining all the small steps needed. To avoid disappointment, be sure to allow ample time. 'Build in time to fail,' recommends Carr. 'Review the steps regularly and change them as necessary.'

REAL PEOPLE

"I discovered my ambition to sing at 38." – *Angie*

'I had a rubbish time when I left college, there's no two ways about it. Basically I didn't know what I wanted to do. I just wanted a job, and I was willing to work hard. Which I did, but I discovered other people were getting paid more than me for doing a lot less work. So I left. This happened about three times; it was the same every time: I'd have my head down, work really hard, be the reliable one, but I always ended up feeling shafted.

Singing was always my thing, I did it at weddings, I loved karaoke and was always in a choir. But I never took it further. People did suggest I should do this professionally but I thought they were being polite. I didn't want to be a pop star, I just loved singing. I just wasn't one of those ambitious people.

I had a year when yet another relationship collapsed, I got made redundant, couldn't find a job, lost the flat I was renting because the landlord wanted it back, and had to move in with my parents. I hit rock bottom and was on anti-depressants. I wasn't even 40 and I was made to feel too old for jobs. I couldn't get myself out of feeling bad no matter what I tried. Thinking positive, visualizing angels, positive affirmations, mindfulness meditation and all that might work for some people, none of it was for me. But I still went to choir. That was what kept me going. That was my therapy. It was the only time I did my hair, put on some make up, got out of my track pants and felt like a person who was alive.

Being honest rather than putting on a front was what helped. Eventually I started really listening to what people were saying: maybe I could train to be a vocal coach, try the Voice or the X Factor for a laugh, or join an agency to sing at weddings. So I thought, right, I'm going to take this seriously and see where it goes. I took courses, joined a choir with a different style, signed up with an agency, and did a skills exchange with a singing coach by doing her accounts and admin. One of my courses is in musical theatre and I absolutely love it. My plan now is to get into the chorus of a musical. I guess that's an ambition! I'm working now at the box office for a musical and although the pay is rubbish I love it, it makes me feel close to my dream. I'm going into my 40s with a passion and a mission.'

ASK YOURSELF

Q What currently drains your mental energy on a daily basis?

Q What would be the easiest and simplest change to make right now in your life?

Q Are you dieting – or are you eating healthily?

Q How can you learn to rest and reenergize more?

Q What do you need to learn to do for maximum wellbeing (to boost maximum willpower)?

CHAPTER 8

WHAT KIND OF SUCCESSFUL PERSON DO YOU WANT TO BE?

You might be thinking: well any success would do. If you've had a tough time, or you've experienced knock backs, then feeling despondent is understandable and normal. You might be wondering why you can't be successful while others seem to have everything.

However, rather than dwelling on this, we want you to consider what kind of successful person you want to be. By being more specific about these details, you can help yourself build that balanced vision of success. You will also discover more versions of success.

LOOK FOR SUCCESS STORIES WHEN YOU'RE FEELING UNSUCCESSFUL

Looking for people who are worse off than you is a natural impulse when you're feeling disappointed with your life – it's official. A 2014 study at Ohio University[1] found that when people are positive they look for 'success-oriented' updates, but when depressed they look for the less successful to make themselves feel better. This has become the modern way to manage moods; however, reading about people you admire and how they created their successful lives is what you need at this point. Instead of feeding your frustration and disappointment with the negative action of searching for less successful people to make you feel better, feed yourself with inspiration, ideas and information.

By forming a picture of the kind of successful person you want to be, you can determine what process your ambition must take. Let's say you are pretty shy but really want to start your own business – a business that would involve you being face to face with lots of people probably isn't a model that will work for you. However, you don't have to change who you are to be successful, you simply have to find the version of success that feels comfortable and exciting for you.

Instead of thinking of success and successful people as some sort of abstract ideal of yourself that you want to achieve, we want to guide you in this chapter to reflect on specific types of people. By forming a more precise idea of the ideal person you would like to be, you can mould your ambitions so that you feel entirely comfortable and at one with this person.

CHRIS BARÉZ-BROWN ON IDENTIFYING WHAT SUCCESS MEANS TO YOU

- *'Ambition and success used to be about materialistic gain – but not anymore. Most of us have all we need in terms of food, shelter, TVs, holidays, so we can choose how we want to live.*

- *Once you've got the basics, you say: Is this it? If I have 33-inch TV, do I need a 36-inch one?*

- *We are way more plugged into information, so our expectations have changed. There is freedom and flexibility.*

- *We are consuming more than the planet can produce and we know that at some point there will be repercussions. People are starting to understand that we can't carry on living the way we are living, yet we can have an influence on changing this way of life.*

> * *For more and more people, ambition is not materialistic for us now. People want money to have more experiences. What experiences would you like to have?*
>
> * *Everyone likes nice stuff but buying more stuff gives us that primal "hunt and kill" endorphin rush. We are becoming conflicted about this which is why brands that do good are becoming more attractive. If a brand is ethical and sustainable, then when we buy them we're doing something good for the planet.'*

CELEBRITIES AND PUBLIC FIGURES

Though social media creates an impression that our society has an unhealthy fascination with and admiration for celebrities, there are indications that not everybody is fooled by the celebrity culture. A 2015 educational study[2] involving six schools with a variety of ethnic and social backgrounds discovered that teenagers admire celebrities who they believe have worked hard, and weren't impressed with those who haven't done much to become famous.

Even if you don't wish to be in the public eye, there's much to be learnt from the information freely available on those who are. This information can help you think about what kind of successful person you'd like to be. More importantly you can decide whether you would enjoy the processes they went through to achieve success, from their training, the hours they worked, their personal relationships, to how they dealt with difficult times. Whether your career ambitions lie in sport, politics, business, the arts, music or reaching the top in a corporate world, there are interesting lessons and parallels to be drawn from these.

For example, Louisa Johnson, the 2015 winner of the X-Factor at just 17, was driven to sing from a child.[3] As a result, her parents sent her to a performing arts school, she had voice coaching lessons, and her life coach mother coached her further towards believing in her success. The show's 2004 winner Alexandra Burke[4] started singing when she was 5 and was performing by the age of 9. When she was rejected by the X-Factor the first time, she went away, improved her skills – and went back to win.

Even if your ambitions have nothing to do with music, what you can see from the X-Factor is that winners don't just turn up and win. They've worked at it. They've had indications in advance that they're on the right path. They've tested out their dream in small ways. In the same way, you can work at it (whatever 'it' is for you), look for the positive feedback to check if you're on the right track, and test out what you want to do in small ways.

Entrepreneurs don't start big. They may try several businesses before the one that takes off. Sir James Dyson developed a staggering 5,126 prototypes for his vacuum cleaner until the 5,127th worked[5] and became the top seller and synonymous with success. It took him 15 years. If you have a business idea, ask yourself how important this is and how much you could strive to develop it. You don't have to go to Dyson's extremes, but if you want to quit before you've even started you have to ask yourself if you truly are committed to your particular idea.

READ MEMOIRS AND BIOGRAPHIES

Seeing how people you admire have lived their journeys to achievement, or how they transformed something in their lives, is a way to find inspiration and learn from their stories in a more in-depth,

> meaningful way than short and superficial media
> interviews. You might discover they had similar
> backgrounds or problems as you. They might
> describe how they dealt with rejection. Their stories
> might entertain you or make you cry and either
> way, by gaining deeper appreciation, you also gain
> strength to continue on your way.

When you're committed to what you value, you become open
to so many possibilities. One of the most iconic international
politicians was one who didn't intend to be a politician but
followed his passion for economics. Yiannis Varoufakis,[6] the
former Greek Finance Minister, is a professor of economics who
studied at Sussex and Birmingham Universities and taught at
universities in the UK, Athens and the USA. In addition to writing
books, he also blogged. From this he found himself the most
photographed politician globally during Greece's most tumultuous
political period since dictatorship. Yet he didn't set out to be
a politician, let alone famous. He remained true to his values,
including travelling to parliament on his motorbike and not
wearing a suit and tie.

We tend to assume when it comes to sport that this has to
be an innate talent, yet the same principles apply here. As
we saw in Chapter 4, talent isn't enough. It's certainly true in
sports where athletes have to train relentlessly. We also saw in
Chapter 4 that true grit is one of the reasons people are most
likely to succeed, and that's certainly apparent in the world of
sport. Michael Jordan might be the world's most well-known
basketball player, yet he didn't make it onto his high school's
team.[7] In the early stages of playing he was also deemed too
short. When you look at how athletes train and maintain their

motivation it's worth asking how you train and maintain your motivation for what it is you want to do.

FINDING POSITIVES IN STEREOTYPES

There's much to be learnt from studying groups of people with the same traits or a representation of a type of person with certain traits. Let's say your ambition is to be a banker. What's the stereotype banker (lawyer/entrepreneur/actor/ whatever you chose for whatever reason) like? What positive qualities are they associated with? What are the negative aspects associated with them? Does the stereotype match your personality in any way? Is it the positive or the negative you match?

If you are part of a group that's stereotyped it's worth asking too what the negatives/positives are for this group. Anything from going to public school to growing up on benefits, being fat or skinny, belonging to a minority ethnic background or having a congenital condition will stereotype you. Yet that needn't be bad news. A *ScienceDaily* report in 2008[8] featured psychologists from the University of Exeter and St Andrews University who argued that stereotypes can affect people negatively *and* positively. 'What we think about ourselves – and also, what we believe others think about us – determines both how we perform and what we are able to become,' said Professor Alex Haslam of the University of Exeter in the interview. Stereotypes can hold you back but, according to Haslam, if you belong to a group stereotyped as the best 'this can promote personal achievement'.

Of course you won't be stereotyping yourself; this is all part of decoding information that can be useful for your journey so that you can create an original imprint of you.

PROFESSOR FORTLOUIS WOOD ON SELF-CRITICISM AND SELF-ASSESSMENT

'One of the missing pieces for many people as they develop into adult roles or make transitions in mid-life is an accurate read on their goals, skills and how they solve problems or navigate their lives. It's not that they are just negative about their prospects, but also that they only examine one part of their life at a time, and do so through the imagined criticisms of others. They look for shortcomings, not strengths. They discount their achievements and compare themselves to people who are unusual or extraordinary in one or more aspects of their lives. And their views of such role models focus only on the outcomes – they rarely consider the costs, losses and sacrifices of those whom they admire.

A realistic assessment of one's strengths and areas for growth is essential. It's important to recognize that one has to make choices and many choices rule out other paths, and there are often important advantages in both paths. In spite of the idea put forward in the media that one can have it all – it's an absurd notion. You can have a full and enriching life with multiple facets and stages – but not everything. There are just too many possibilities. We should think about our choices from a resource perspective and recognize that there are always trade-offs.

Personality, energy level, health, financial status and stage in life are all important factors to consider. Bear in mind that there is a great deal of variability between individuals and you cannot simply mimic the choices of people around you – they may have very different goals, values, resources and temperaments.'

WHICH ARCHETYPE ARE YOU?

Looking at archetypes is one of the most effective tools for finding real ambition. Think of archetypes as prototypes – the first and original model of a particular person.

In psychoanalysis this concept originated with Carl Jung.[9] As we saw in Chapter 3, Jung believed each of us has a unique calling that's connected to our purpose in the world at large, or what he termed the 'collective unconscious'. According to Jung, this collective unconscious consists of archetypes we all recognize because they represent basic human behaviour and conditions. We all know, for example, what being a father, mother, child, involves. Jung believed we each have an archetype imprint from birth – and this gives us our purpose, and our place within the collective unconscious.

PROFESSOR FORTLOUIS WOOD ON THE IDEA OF HAVING A CALLING

'The idea that we each have a calling means that we have some obligation to discover what motivates us and allows us to be the best version of ourselves. Although this is hardly a single theme or idea about the self, thinking about our calling or callings allows us to emphasize the work and experiences that we find most fulfilling. By following what inspires us, we are more likely to make contributions that are grounded in deeper motivation and a willingness to work hard and bring projects to fruition. This makes us more valuable to the workplace, committee, our families and community organizations.

In contrast, pursuing goals primarily because others think they matter or because they "look good" may preclude finding a similar goal that actually fits our own motives and values. It's not that you should never do what other people

> *suggest or want (that's unrealistic), but it is important to find*
> *room for exploring what intrigues, inspires and fuels you.*
> *That kind of motivation is often trivialized as selfish. Again, it*
> *is a matter of finding the right balance.'*

Professor of Psychology and licensed clinical psychologist
Lisa Fortlouis Wood is keen to point out that this need not be
connected with a paid job or even make sense, referring us to
psychoanalyst Stella Adler and her work on each individual having
an individual creative force.

What does this mean? In Chapter 3 we listed finding a calling as
being a part of your real ambition. Now you can see too that by
tapping into this you are doing your bit for the universe. But your
calling can take many forms. Think of that barista every morning
who makes you feel a teeny bit special by remembering your
name and taking a few seconds to greet you in a real way. Think
of that family member who has the knack of making everyone feel
welcome at absolutely any time. Think of that person who has
everyone in stitches at work. For some people a creative force will
come through their personality and the way they can make others
feel good. It doesn't matter what job they do. A calling or a creative
force doesn't have to be about being rich or famous or successful
in a creative field. Once you figure it out, you can transform the
energy you bring to your job, whether that's law or insurance, and
you can infuse every area of your life with this energy.

66 Each person can actualize their own calling by tapping into the experiences they find most motivating and inspiring. 99

Lisa Fortlouis Wood, Professor of Psychology and licensed
clinical psychologist

Jung's archetypes were further developed by author and archetype expert Carol S. Pearson:[10] The Innocent, the Regular Guy/Gal, the Warrior/Hero, the Caregiver, the Explorer, the Outlaw, the Lover, the Creator, the Ruler, the Magician, the Sage, the Jester. Even without going into significant detail about each archetype, they may feel familiar. You know deep down which ones you most definitely are not, and which one or two resonate as you read through the list.

Headhunter, coach and author John Purkiss and his co-author David Royston-Lee take this model a step further in *Brand You.*[11] The book's powerful premise is that to be successful we need to project what's unique about us by developing our personal brand – how we can be remembered and make our mark. One of the tools the authors use in their model for personal branding is archetypes. In workshops all over the world they have found that people recognize the same archetypes:

> *'Our starting point is that you have a purpose. Developing a powerful brand involves projecting your purpose to the outside world [...] If your behaviour is consistent with your natural archetype(s), your brand will take on a meaning that increases your appeal to people who want what you have to offer.'*[12]

The thing is, you can't choose an archetype. If you'd like to be creative you can't simply decide the Creator is your archetype. You have to ask yourself if you do naturally feel compelled to create – whether that's music or new products.

How you see yourself and how others see you can be different too. As Purkiss further explains:

> *'You may see a certain archetype or archetypes in yourself. Other people may see different archetypes in you. If so, it's important (a) to ensure that the archetype you see in yourself is not wishful thinking, and (b) to change the image you project to others, so that you and they see the same archetypes in you.'*

The archetypes are summed up by Purkiss and Royston-Lee in their book *Brand You* below.[13] Take a look and see what resonates most with you and your ambitions:

The Caregiver	Helps and protects from harm
The Creator	Compelled to create and innovate
The Explorer	Explores and discovers
The Hero	Acts courageously to put things right
The Innocent	Seeks purity, goodness and happiness
The Jester	Has a good time but may convey a serious message
The Lover	Finds and gives love and sensual pleasure
The Magician	Transforms situations
The Ordinary Guy/Girl	Ok as they are; connect with others
The Outlaw	Rebels and breaks the rules
The Ruler	Takes control; creates order out of chaos
The Sage	Helps people to understand their world

KELE BAKER ON FINDING YOUR JOURNEY THROUGH ARCHETYPAL JOURNEYS ON TV

'Competitive shows cast a variety of "types" to make interesting viewing so there will be a range of types from brashly ambitious to shy.

We can use American scholar Joseph Campbell's idea that every story features an archetypal Hero's Journey. From a storytelling perspective, the contestants are archetypes on a *journey. The journey appears to be an outward journey, but the really juicy journey is the inward one.*

The desire to achieve something in the outside world (like winning a show) becomes a journey of emotional discovery. The archetypes encounter outer obstacles and have to transcend inner obstacles.

- *Which inner journeys can you identify from a show you are watching? Does the one who lacks confidence get more confident or collapse under pressure? Does the cocky one become humble? Who is enjoying the process regardless of the outcome? What is the inner story for each journey?*
- *In your Hero's Journey, what are your inner obstacles? Fear of speaking up? Lack of courage?*
- *Do you want your goal enough to transcend the obstacles?'*

The kind of successful person you want to be is linked to the kind of person you are right now, inside-out. There's nothing abstract about the central question in this chapter. Far from asking you to pluck out your future qualities as a successful person, we've encouraged you to look at people widely and to search for role models of success who match who you are. Even being part of a group that's stereotyped can give you some valuable pointers. Finding an archetype that fits you can give you a clear template as well as reinforcing whether your inner and outer selves match. From people you know to people you don't know there is ample inspiration out there for you to form a clear idea of your ideal real you and, most importantly, the journey that suits you best

REAL PEOPLE

"I spent a few years soul-searching to find what I really wanted in life." *– David*

'I've always been ambitious, but I've changed how I view ambition. I've been through the whole cycle of being driven to make money, running successful businesses, settling down and getting married – and then realizing I was miserable, drinking too much, feeling I had no real identity.

My favourite game as a kid was making money. I had little businesses going from the playground, selling sweets and comics that I'd buy cheap and sell for double. I dropped out of university because I felt stifled and my parents were so disappointed and ashamed. I then wanted to prove them wrong and to become really successful – which I did running two businesses, one in cleaning and one in flooring, then another repairing windows. They considered that with my private education I could have done better than cleaning and building. My brother became a lawyer and they were proud of him.

I got married because I thought it was the right thing to do. However, I was just going through the motions to keep my ex-wife happy because I loved her and sadly this led to our eventual divorce. I felt so guilty that I was destroying my ex-wife's dreams. But it was the catalyst for me to spend a few years soul searching and really working out what I wanted from life.

I sold up all my businesses after the divorce and decided to have a year off to travel around the world, like a gap year in middle age. It turned into two years. My father died just before I went and it turned out he felt very proud of me, not because of my financial achievements but for the fact that I did it my way. He had been a corporate workaholic with heart problems.

I know now that it's not money as such that drives me – I'm not materialistic. It's the freedom and independence that drives me. When I was a kid I could make money to buy things or do things we weren't allowed to do or had to ask permission for. I realized through therapy that my relationships were always with women who needed me and were dependent on me so I felt suffocated. I thought this meant relationships are not for me. It took me a while to own up to preferring a close loving relationship than lots of lovers. I'm with someone I love very much now, and I'm learning to be me and to be loving.

I've been meditating and practising mindfulness for some time now. I check in with myself every day and I try to be as honest with myself as I can. I still see myself as ambitious but my ambition is about creating a life that's good for me; I look for everything from how I make money to who I am with to bring out the best in me. If I'm distracted, drinking too much, bored, insensitive, restless, depressed, I've learnt there's something to address.'

ASK YOURSELF

Q Who are your favourite pop stars, politicians, athletes, actors, entrepreneurs? What are the qualities you admire in them? What lesson can you learn from each one from their journey to success?

Q Which TV programmes can you use to help you discover inspiring inner journeys?

Q Who will be your role models for success?

Q If you could create a completely new way of living your life, what would it be?

CHAPTER 9

FIVE SIMPLE SECRETS TO SUCCESS

I n Chapter 6, we identified 10 ambition traps which all came down to identifying how to avoid falling into unhelpful thought patterns. It's not your fault if you have fallen into these thought patterns, because they are all around us. We've given you short tips throughout the book that will boost your way to success, and plenty of specific advice from our experts.

The great thing about the secrets in this chapter is that you don't need to worry about whether you are capable of achieving them – just think of them as simple directions to follow so that your journey goes smoothly. Using these five simple secrets you will be able to further develop your willpower and strengthen your motivation to achieve your ambitions. Eventually you'll find that implementing all the advice we've given you so far will come easily.

1. GO WITH THE FLOW

" Find a wave that helps you, and ride it. "

Chris Baréz-Brown, creative and business beatnik

To date, there are roughly two schools of thought on success. One is based on deciding on your goal(s) and working hard to make these happen, no matter what. The other is based on visualizing your dream, thinking positively and believing success will come to you because you deserve it. You may have tried either or both these ways already. For some people, maybe these methods work. The problem is they don't work for everyone. If you've been lucky to hit on an ambition that fits your psychological make-up, your natural aptitudes and strengths, and you're in an environment where this is possible, then either of these might work. But for most people there is more trial and error.

Instead of trial and error we suggest a different approach: enter and try-it-all.

When you arrive in an exciting new city you will probably have downloaded a couple of apps, and researched the places that most interest you. You'll have an idea of what you want to see and where you want to go. You want to make the most of your time in London or Paris or New York because you know that if you arrive with zero planning, your time will easily be frittered away. But of course, you don't want a clockwork plan, hour by hour, you allow for spontaneity too. Your approach to a city break is the one you need for your life too: a plan that allows for spontaneity, change and adventure. Just because a bar is on your list because it's rated number one on Trip Advisor doesn't mean you have to stay there if it's too crowded when you arrive, you don't feel like cocktails anyway – and you spot a pop up bar-restaurant that's not even listed yet across the road.

KELE BAKER ON FLOW VS PUSH

'Chinese philosophy refers us to the natural flow of nature. If a boulder falls into a river, the river gets jammed up. On one side of the bank there is too much water so it is muddy, swamped and stagnant. The land on the other side is dry and deficient. When we get rid of the boulder, the river flows and balance returns. Water flows naturally; it doesn't have to be forced anywhere. If your ambition is a river, what block can you identify? Where in your life are you flowing? Where in your life are you pushing? Why are you pushing – what are you pushing?

The Chinese principle of Yin and Yang is based on the dynamic and complementary balance of opposing energies. Yang is the *"make-it-happen" energy, and yin is the "allow-things-to-flow-and-happen" energy. Can you identify this in your life?*

Sometimes we need to do more – sometimes we need to make an effort. And sometimes we need to sit back and see what's flowing in our lives at the moment. What's flowing in your life right now?

If we're constantly trying, working hard and feeling no sense of appreciation, then we become frustrated and even distraught. Where in your life can you go easy on yourself?

Assess regularly where you're at, and what you're doing. Ask yourself: are things flowing and happening, or am I trying too hard to make things happen?

When you encounter an obstacle, assess the obstacle. How do you want to handle it? Can you go over it, around it, or dig a tunnel under it? Or is it too big an obstacle and not worth trying to overcome? Is it more beneficial to flow in a different direction?

When the pieces in your life seem to fit together, you feel confident that the timing is right. If you are coming across too many obstacles, and feeling unable to handle these, ask yourself: is the timing right?

Flow is a dynamic interplay of "doing" and "allowing". It's never just one or the other – it's both, but in ever-changing amounts, thereby creating a sense of overall balance and harmony.

Flow in life feels light, easy and effortless. There is no struggle or drama. You feel good about what you're doing.'

2. SET COMPLEMENTARY GOALS

As we saw in Chapter 7, how you set goals is crucial to your success and is an important aspect of learning to be ambitious. Remember, the key is to choose goals that gear you up to taking action now towards a future goal. Since real ambition is multidimensional, we want to address setting goals in different areas of your life.

One of the problems with setting goals is getting too focused on the individual elements without seeing them as one. One goal is to get promoted at work (which means working overtime). Another goal is to go for coffee with three different people from three different dating sites every week (which involves spending time online sifting through profiles, making contact, establishing a rapport and making an arrangement). Well that's not going to work is it? What's more the goals will cancel each other out so you end up not doing one or the other.

ALLOCATE TIME FOR YOUR MUNDANE TASKS

We know from the guru of willpower, Baumeister, that procrastination is a major block to willpower. But it's not just putting off taking big actions to make big changes. There are also all sorts of mundane tasks you are probably putting off, such as household tasks, filling in forms or sorting out your computer. The problem is these mundane tasks still take up mental energy, even if you're not doing them. They're there nagging you. And they stop you taking the major action you need to take. Instead of letting the boring things pile up, allocate short bursts of time to deal with these. Start with committing to five minutes a day. Break down every boring task so that it can be done bit by bit if need be. Look for windows of dead time – from commercial breaks when you're watching TV, to lunch breaks at work that are frittered away. Plan to use these time-windows and watch how light, empowered and motivated you feel as a result.

Professor of Psychology and licensed clinical psychologist Lisa Fortlouis Wood favours using the wheel of life method to mark where you're at and where you'd like to be. First, draw a circle and divide it into the different areas of your life. Write down how things are now and what you'd like to achieve. Once completed, you can see clearly everything that's within the circle. Then you always have your wheel of life to remind you of all the areas in your life where things are going well, areas that might get forgotten, as well as spotting where there might be conflict.

It's the master of willpower who advises that we set complementary goals. Baumeister[1] refers to a 1988 Michigan State university study,[2] which found that when people set conflicting goals their health is affected, they worry more and get less done. When we interviewed Baumeister for *Psychologies* magazine,[3] he affirmed his advice on setting aside a day every year to reflect, having a 'vague' five-year objective, thinking in terms of major goals, and then making specific intermediate goals through monthly plans.

PROFESSOR FORTLOUIS WOOD ON GAINING PERSPECTIVE VIA 360 DEGREE GOALS ASSESSMENT

'The wheel is one way to assess goals in several areas of life. You can divide it into work, relationships, leisure, where you live (plus any additional section you would like to choose) and identify the specific goals you are working on for each category, and the behaviours/actions that move you forward.

Knowing your goals, together with your values, resources and strengths makes a decision process more accurate in terms of matching your individual profile to any area in your life.

You can also create a detailed work and relationship history with specifics on skills and lessons learned in each experience. This can lead you to a valuable set of self-statements around your strengths and how you have arrived where you are.

This kind of exploration is useful for those in mid-life work or relationship transitions, as well as retirement transitions.'

3. FIND LIKE-MINDED PEOPLE

One of the things that might be dragging you down is a feeling that one way or another you are surrounded by people who don't understand you. At one end of the scale perhaps all your friends are sailing through their careers or getting married, and you feel left behind. Or maybe all your friends are moaning about no opportunities, relationships being rubbish, and you feel they're all dragging you down. You may be somewhere in between, experiencing both and feeling there is something wrong with you.

The thing is, if we go back to the pure meaning of ambition, it's about striving for a desire. This immediately indicates that you want something different. It doesn't matter what that is. If all your friends like Chinese food and you hate it, will going for a Chinese meal with them every week make you like it? If you used to like Indian takeaways but ever since you got a dodgy tummy you can't stand the smell, and your partner insists on ordering Indian takeaways, are you going to like them again? In both scenarios you will feel exasperated, annoyed, angry, fed up. It's the same with anything else in your life.

There is ample research that shows being with like-minded people is crucial. It's what psychologists refer to as contagious willpower. Think about support groups from Alcoholics Anonymous to Weight Watchers. People find it easier to give something up within a group of individuals they can connect with.

> **66 Hang out with people who are more ambitious and brave than you – who you hang out with does influence who you become, so if you are safe and timid and risk averse ... 99**

Chris Baréz-Brown, creative and business beatnik

One of the biggest studies on the subject was by Nicholas Christakis at Harvard Medical School and James Fowler at University of California San Diego.[4] They looked at the Framingham Heart Study which tracked the lives of 12,000 residents for 32 years, with intimate details of their lives. Christakis and Fowler found that obesity and drinking are contagious. But so is giving up smoking. Their research concluded that we have an in-built instinct to mirror others around us. Happiness, they found, spread from friend to friend.

There's just one snag that psychologists have identified when it comes to goal contagion. You can't catch new goals. If all your friends want to make the maximum amount of money in the least amount of time and are taking jobs in sales or in finance, while you want to study a new skill so that you can set up a business, they won't 'catch' your goal. You, however, might be 'infected' because as a group they will be on the same wavelength, boosting each other. This will undermine you. To strengthen your ambition you need to find others who are also studying a new skill and aspiring to set up a business. And you also need people who are further along the line who can be healthy role models and even mentors.

DANNIE-LU CARR ON HANDLING FAMILY AND FRIENDSHIPS

- *'Put yourself on the priority list, and not at the bottom of it. This doesn't mean you won't be there for family, but you want to be in charge of how much energy you give to family, and you want to avoid falling for entrenched family dynamics.*

- *Learn to set boundaries rather than keep people happy. Decide on your boundaries, make these clear, and stick to them. When you are with family be completely present – this is what will make them happy. That way when you're working on your own thing, they won't resent you.*

- *Be honest with yourself about friendships. Do certain people drain you? Do certain people knock you off-centre or distract you from what you really want to do? Trust your gut feelings. You don't have to take everyone on*

board. If you have to let go of friends, allow yourself time
to grieve for the loss.

* **Speak out your truth but avoid conflict.** Soften what
you want to say with "it might be that you …". Level the
playing field.

* **Be watchful of who is around you.** Does their presence
support your goals? Do they actively support your goals?

* **Focus on learning how a friendship can work for you.** If a
night out drinking isn't good for you say: "I'd rather spend
time with you over lunch", or, "I'd rather go to the park
with you".'

4. KNOW THE DIFFERENCE BETWEEN LIKE AND WANT

Surely they're more or less the same thing? Why would anyone
want what they don't like? Why would anyone not want what they
like? When you watch a toddler it's obvious that they have definite
don't-likes. They spit out vegetables, they won't go on the slides,
they refuse a spoon and won't wear the orange shoes. As we
move from childhood to adolescence to adulthood all sorts of
things happen: we become conditioned by our environment, we
cover up our feelings to please others, we're swamped with choice
and we also fall into routines.

If you rush out to work every day and gobble up some cereal
because it's easy, you might have never thought about whether you
like it or want it until you go on holiday and discover eating pineapple
for breakfast excites you, or having scrambled eggs sets you up
really well for the day and you don't snack on rubbish. It's easier to
consider tangible things and figure out like/want. Once you click into
asking yourself the question at every point you will notice all sorts

of shifts. You will be drawn to healthier food, for example, as you realize that no, you don't want the unhealthy fast food, and yes, you kind of like burgers and fries but not really because you feel bloated and heavy afterwards. Being mindful of a habit like eating fast food will motivate you to at least try a healthy food chain so that you shift your taste buds and habits gradually and effectively.

When it comes to our inner world, however, the process becomes more challenging. Yes, it can be deeply uncomfortable and strange. But we can promise you it's also exciting. From the small details in your life to the complete picture, working out like vs want maximizes your ability to achieve your vision of success.

KELE BAKER ON THE POWER OF LIKE

'What do I like?

Asking yourself what you like gives you the feeling of having it already. Asking yourself what you want implies something you don't have, something that's outside of you.

For every outward ambition check inward first. How does what you want fit with what you like now?

If the ambition is to buy a first property, ask yourself exactly why? What would buying a property satisfy? Is there a should involved? Are all your friends wanting this? Do you need security or an investment? When you are exactly clear, this helps you consider different options.

Use what you like to find what you want. Be mindful about what you like and be open about how everything you like will come together. By being focused on what you like you become open to ideas. We don't always know what we want because we may not know it exists.'

5. THINK FEASIBLE

What? Feasible? Isn't that boring? Isn't that consigning your dreams to the bin and telling you to keep calm and carry on? Have we tricked you into reading this far only to tell you it's all one big lie? Absolutely not. We could have chosen a different word, like realistic or strategic. We like the word feasible, however, because in-built in this word is the idea that something will happen, it'll work out, it'll be real.

Unfortunately many people let their fantasies get out of hand. As Gabriele Oettingen outlines in her book *Rethinking Positive Thinking – Inside the New Science of Motivation*[5] 'fantasies only deplete efforts and lead us to stumble over and over again'. Oettingen has been researching fantasy since the nineties, and with her colleagues has conducted detailed studies in Germany and the US on how dreaming about a goal affects achieving it. From shoes to weight, studying to dating, the research arrives at the same conclusion: dreaming about achieving a goal can actually get in the way completely.

As Oettingen explains in the book, there's a difference between being optimistic based on your experiences, which might lead to positive expectations, and what she calls 'free-flowing thought and images rooted in wishes and desires'. Oettingen refers not only to her own research but to other studies demonstrating that day dreaming can be a coping mechanism that helps get you through a boring day, but there is no long-term benefit. 'Our dreams may be realizable,' she writes, 'but they come down to challenges that require engagement and action.'

So, you need to be engaged with your dream – that means you must feel truly energized and excited, enough to want to take action. Psychologists have studied the bit in between your intentions and actions, and refer to it as implementation-intentions. Oettingen's husband in fact has conducted studies on this.[6] The key is one word: plan.

You can't plan without being realistic. Realistic doesn't mean negative. When your mind throws up all the obstacles in your way, being negative is insisting that you've no hope. But if you believed that, you wouldn't be reading this book. Being realistic involves being creative about what you need to do, how, and even when.

PROFESSOR FORTLOUIS WOOD ON TAKING TIME TO FIGURE THINGS OUT

'When one considers the idea of ambition, one ought to recognize that a beeline towards gratification of an immediate goal (eating at the first restaurant on the list in the guidebook; or the one someone recommends) may circumvent a process of researching, exploring and deciding that teaches many important lessons. Getting lost is exceedingly valuable in learning terrain – following the well-travelled path, though expedient, is often much less instructive.

Consider what happens when you ask someone where to eat, or what art exhibit to visit, or what to read? Typically they tell you what they like or what they did. If they are similar to you, that information can be very valuable. But often, too often, another individual's goals, values, aesthetic tastes and experiences are not well aligned with yours. Further, they may not have any real idea of what is out there beyond whatever they have experienced; perhaps they are following patterns laid down by others, or what they read in the paper – places that are often advertised for a fee. Most importantly, they may not have much idea about your goals and interests.

Stumbling around for a while may give a much broader sample of what is available – especially if one has a nose for where to look. So, although efficiency and expediency may lead to adequate and sometimes excellent outcomes, doing your own exploration and research is also essential. Either way, there's no guarantee of the right fit; that takes time to figure out. Often it is the missing ingredient for people – taking time to do their own research; taking time to consider what fits and discovering what kinds of experiences are most valuable in relation to their specific goals. Taking time to reflect, evaluate and plan – a key ingredient.'

Going with the flow, setting complementary goals, being with like-minded people, knowing the difference between like and want, and thinking about what's feasible will lead you to success without exhausting you and without you giving up. By this stage you are equipped to embrace these five simple secrets because we have steered you away from success based on old-style ambition. You'll be able to go with the flow because your thinking has shifted away from ambition being associated with hard-edged no-matter-what attitudes. You'll be able to set complementary goals because you will be focusing on developing ambitions that match your inner needs. As part of this you'll be looking to be with like-minded people who share your values and approach to life because you've also learnt that this is crucial to maximizing your willpower. Your awareness now of your inner needs means you will be tuned in to what you like right now. And being rooted in the now will help you plan in a way that's realistic so that your goals are feasible – in other words achievable. With these five simple secrets you can build your way to a success that's not a fantasy or an unimaginable dream. With these five simple secrets you can start to build small successes into your life now.

REAL PEOPLE

"A vase the price of my wages changed my life." *– Kris*

'When I came to this country 15 years ago I was too young, with no experience to think what I want for myself and to make this happen.

I was learning English and working in a coffee chain in a shopping mall. I was so happy to be in a British city. When I looked at my first wage slip I was standing outside a shop window in the mall. There was a vase which cost the same amount as my wages. I thought to myself: for some people this is just a vase. So I told myself: you must make something in your life, not just spend it on beer. The vase made me do my English homework. I spoke to every customer to practise my English. I did not complain about working in the coffee shop. I took another job in a pub so I could practise speaking and have free beer at the weekend.

My landlord found out I was fixing things in the house and asked me to work for him helping and fixing things for tenants. He was pleased with my work because everybody liked me and I liked to fix problems. Nothing was a problem for me. When I finished my English language course he said I should learn to be a plumber and electrician and with this British qualification I will always work. So I did. I didn't have to look for a job, my landlord had plenty of work for me when I qualified. He became a friend and I learnt a lot from him.

The next course I did was in accounting, even though I hate mathematics. I also took a course in computers which gave me confidence to have my own business. When I set up my own company it was a big moment. I had my own staff and my own clients. It took 10 years working hard to arrive here. It was now me taking friends out with my car and buying drinks so they could impress women. But for me I did not want a woman who sees only my car and orders drinks. There was someone who loved me, so I proposed to my girlfriend.

Now I am married, with our first child on the way; we have our own house, and I have a very good business. Last year I organized for my company to put in new central heating for a hospice and I also paid for its refurbishment. This gave me big satisfaction.

In my country people say "oh you are very successful", but this is because they see my wife looks beautiful, we have a home and a car in England as well as in our country. They see the outside.

For me I am successful because I wake up every day with a lot of energy and I go to sleep every night smiling and with joy. I am the boy who was not clever or handsome at school, with no particular talent. Everybody said: "oh he is the nice one, the kind one, he is too nice, too kind". I am happy that I can be successful without changing inside.

I often think of the vase and the moment I decided to make something in my life.'

ASK YOURSELF

Q How does my ego get in the way?

Q Which area(s) in my life are blocked?

Q What part does money play in my vision of ambition and success?

Q Do I have conflicting or complementary goals?

Q Who in my life thinks and feels like me?

Q What do I like today?

CHAPTER 10

KEEPING TRACK OF YOUR AMBITIONS EVERY DAY

W hen you began to read this book you wanted to find out how to achieve your dream of success. We've hopefully guided you to a different vision of success based on aligning what you truly want inside with what you do on the outside. Our experts from their different perspectives have agreed that striving for whatever benefits your inner self is the key to real ambition and success.

By reflecting on what kind of success you want as well as what kind of successful person you want to be, you will have a more accurate sense of who and what you aspire to. We hope that as a result of completing the Ask Yourself questions and the tests throughout, you feel optimistic. You don't have to change who you are and become a certain type of person. Sure, you may have to do some work on certain limiting beliefs, you will have to create a plan of action; but actually, we're confident you can do that. Throughout this book we've given you tips to boost your ambition in the form of simple advice that can make a big difference to your mental outlook. We wanted to encourage you from the beginning to take small actions because it's the combination and the cumulative effect of these small actions that builds your resolve to make big decisions.

In this section we're going to take you through your daily and weekly routines, through to public holidays and vacations. Ambition isn't something you can leave until the weekend after the week when you felt so miserable that you made a pact to make a whole load of goals. You probably already know that doesn't work – you're tired, you've got a whole load of dirty washing to sort out, the fridge is empty, and you desperately need cheering up. You probably already know making a long list of New Year's resolutions doesn't work either.

That's why in this section we tackle real life so that you are prepared and set up. There is absolutely no reason to blame yourself or feel bad about yourself. You have every reason to experience difficulties – but now you have the know-how to deal with these. You need daily awareness to put together the concepts of ambition, willpower, drive, dreams, success, achievements, accomplishments, happiness, fulfillment, joy, satisfaction and inner peace.

WHEN YOU GET UP

How you start the day is crucial. We could add, how you start the day is crucial to how you live the rest of your life, but that might sound too dramatic, right? If you've had a late night, put your alarm on snooze several times, get dressed and out of the door in a mad rush, grab caffeine and sugar to sustain you, how good are you feeling? Yet when you're on holiday, you get up relaxed, you have that nice hotel buffet breakfast that includes lots of fruit and an omelette made to order, and you get out into the sun onto the beach and feel total clarity about your life.

> **"As soon as you get out of bed, sit quietly for ten minutes on your own somewhere and connect with yourself and nature. Take this time to clear your head."**
>
> Chris Baréz-Brown, creative and business beatnik

The fact is, if you have a rushed start to the day you will feel bad all day and not have the head space to make changes so that you can have better days and the life you want. You don't need to do anything drastic. We're not insisting that you get up and meditate or bake eggs in avocados or do anything you don't want to do.

Find the optimum time to go to bed so you can get up without rushing. When you wake up, give yourself a few minutes at least to just be with you – not emails, not social media, not the news, just be with you.

DURING YOUR DAY

Whether you have a job that is far from your dream job, or you're struggling to get onto a career ladder, or perhaps you're at home with a baby or small children, your thoughts and actions during the day have an impact on your future days. It's very easy to get caught in a rut and it's natural to find it hard to climb out of that rut.

> **"Make what you've got today better. Or change it. Don't get stuck on thinking that the grass is greener somewhere else. Perfection doesn't exist."**
>
> Chris Baréz-Brown, creative and business beatnik

Here's where you need to be aware of not letting yourself spiral into negative thinking but instead taking practical actions that will act as a buffer between you and the rut. Remind yourself, for example, of the various tips we've given you throughout the book and make a point of putting one into practice during the day. You could also make a conscious point of becoming aware and changing something you've identified as robbing your motivation.

When we looked at how willpower works in Chapter 7 as part of whether you can learn to be ambitious, we highlighted the importance of nutrition in building willpower. This is where you have the practical chance to put that into practice: dieting or eating junk food does not build your willpower muscle. Simply by eating healthily you help yourself stay out of the mental rut and routine rut. By directing your mind to eating healthily you are diverting it away from negative thoughts that bring you down.

CHRIS BARÉZ-BROWN'S TIPS ON HOW TO HAVE A GOOD DAY

- *'Manage your distraction: turn off your email, app, and social media notifications. We are constantly nagged by information and what happens is that our cognitive process gets shallower. We don't deal with real issues because we're switched on to too many issues. By turning off notifications you enable yourself to deal with these when you want to and at the right time.*

- *Nail it: have in your mind that one thing you've decided to nail for the day. Do it.*

- *Vary your state: get up and get away from your desk. Don't sit doing the same thing for too long. Look after your energy. Be aware of your environment. Feed yourself well. Consider who you are with. Nothing else will work if you don't get you feeling right.*

- *Treat your job the same way you approach buying clothes: try different things. Ask colleagues and bosses to let you try out doing something new rather than being resigned to disliking what you do. Think of the process as like trying on different clothes until you find what fits.*

- *Start small: small actions lead to big visions. Many businesses start with one person making one thing for fun first.'*

WHENEVER YOU DEAL WITH PEOPLE

At this point you might be thinking it's all very well setting yourself up with good habits, but as soon as you speak to your colleague/ boss/partner/mother you get really wound up and can't recover unless you have a coffee/doughnut/alcohol. We totally understand that. But are you going to let other people get in the way of your life by upsetting you? Aren't you worth more than that? Yes, yes, yes, but, but, but, you're saying. We don't need to hear the specifics of why your colleagues annoy you, why your boss makes you feel useless, how your family undermine you, how your partner lets you down, how your best friend ignores you when another friend is around. We understand. We'd like you to 'hear' that it's essential to plan how to handle all these situations.

Creative and business beatnik Chris Baréz-Brown's simple advice is to work out whether you can *avoid* difficult people altogether, simply *accept* the situation by achieving some understanding as to where their behaviour comes from, or *adapt*. 'With some people you may need to change the relationship,' he says. 'Consider how you might do this, try different ways, ask for advice – but be sure to change something.'

Handling friends in particular can be difficult because your friends might be your support system for people giving you a hard time at work or within your family. It's not always possible to spot that certain friends are affecting you negatively. When friends fear losing you they can, without even realizing it, try to pull you away from your plan. However, who you spend your time with, as we saw in Chapter 9, is one of the simple secrets to success. If you're feeling agitated or drained or upset by any friend, rather than feeling guilty and disloyal, accept this is how you feel. A true friendship will survive change and that includes seeing less of a friend because you need to spend time nurturing your ambitions by taking action. Whether you have a central ambition or a general desire to create a successful life on all fronts, you know having read this book that it's a process that requires action – and support.

RECHARGE EVERY DAY

Recharging physically and mentally every day is essential to building the energy, stamina, willpower, resilience and grit you need to achieve rather than just dream. Remember that athletes give their recharging periods as much attention as their training. Recharging really does mean recharging. If you're reading work emails while on the treadmill in the gym you are simply kidding yourself. You're neither looking after your body or your mind.

The challenge with recharging is that we live in a society that loves to be busy. We've become accustomed to watching TV while online with a tablet and replying to messages and emails on our smartphones.

CHRIS BARÉZ-BROWN ON BUSY-NESS BLOCKING SUCCESS

'Busy-ness is habit forming: being busy creates an endorphin kick so the brain loves this. But when it becomes a habit your brain becomes easily bored when not stimulated, so you fill up your diary and run your life being busy. Then on holiday you don't know what to do with yourself.

Busy-ness is highly addictive: when you're busy you feel needed and important.

Busy-ness reduces your awareness: when people are running from one thing to the next they can't remember what they're doing and they're not fully present with whatever they are doing.

Busy-ness becomes an identity: if you take on a busy identity then this will feel like the only way to be successful.'

REWIRE YOUR MIND EVERY DAY

No doubt you're aware of the chatter in your mind that reminds you where you're at now, where you'd like to be, and how others around you are doing. In addition you may be surrounded by colleagues and friends moaning. We're bombarded by news which often isn't pleasant, to say the least. And you may also have financial worries or family members who are sick. This is life. All this is normal. Staying on top of life and being focused on creating the best life for you requires safeguarding your mind, protecting it so you are not drained. The bigger the changes you are aiming to make, and the more obstacles you are overcoming, the more focused you need to be.

If you came to this book because you feel you've had a hard time and you feel down every day, clearly you have decided to change this. This means making sure every day you are creating something good. Today. Now. If you have a bad day in a job that you loathe, you need to find an activity that you enjoy, like learning or practising a skill that will lead to the job that's right for you. If you go on a disastrous date, you need to laugh about it rather than insist there's no one out there for you.

Find a way to rewire your brain every day that works for you. We're not prescriptive about what this is. It could be mindfulness meditation, positive affirmations, cognitive behaviour therapy techniques, listening to a playlist with pop songs that boost you – whatever works for you.

 ## LEARN TO MEDITATE

Meditation is a like a workout for the mind. Studies[1] show that learning to meditate helps the brain get better at a wide range of self-control skills including

attention, focus, stress management, impulse control and self-awareness. Meditation increases the neural connections between regions of the brain which are important for staying focused. An increased blood flow to the prefrontal cortex of the brain (the control system hub for willpower) boosts the brain's ability to be ambitious.

CONNECT FOR REAL

It's become all too easy to kid ourselves that we are connecting with people through social media. But if you're in a job you don't like (or don't have a job), you live far from family, your friends are scattered around and it's not easy to meet, you might not be making real connections with people. And this connection is essential to nurture the willpower you need to achieve your ambitions and create success. Regardless of whether we are loners or party-goers, all human beings need to be part of something bigger to thrive.

In one study, Professor of Psychology and licensed clinical psychologist Lisa Fortlouis Wood gives as an example a communal village community that might be producing fabric, with all the villagers cooperating together. The buzzwords in such a scenario are interdependence, collaboration and mutual trust on a daily basis. In simple terms, everyone pulls together and helps out in emergencies – but they also celebrate together. The research[2] makes it clear that being flexible as well as open to what's going on in our communities or workplaces or any given situation leads to trust and connection. As Professor Fortlouis Wood writes: '[…] it is crucial to have informal gatherings outside of work, where team members can develop personal connections with one another, and see each other in the context of a wider range of social roles and identities.'

Translated into working for a corporation and being part of a team, this means don't skip lunch or drinks because you hate your job. Make your current situation better by finding a small way to connect now. Before you sigh because you're thinking you can't stand your colleagues, this isn't about getting mindlessly drunk with everyone and suffering networking. Make it your mission to find at least one person who feels the same way as you or has a similar temperament or similar interests rather than dismissing everybody. Don't fall into the trap of moaning and gossiping, do something fun or constructive.

PROFESSOR FORTLOUIS WOOD ON BELONGING AND SUCCESS

'We don't survive alone. Being part of something bigger is at the heart of being human.

Women tend to be better than men at creating informal social support structures like book clubs, mothers' clubs, gym classes, but such social endeavours are important for everyone, whether through family and local community, the workplace, religious or spiritual groups, sports or other activities. These groups are important for sharing ideas and information, for giving and receiving help and support when needed, and for attaining a sense of belonging.

We can see the importance for social support, especially when people retire or are laid off from work. Suddenly, an individual is faced with at least 40 hours a week that are no longer structured. Moreover, they lose the sense of belonging, and their identity as a member of the workplace and work group. Without this daily social structure it's easy to feel isolated and without purpose. The challenge is to find another group structure where one can invest in new activities which in time will provide a new identity.

> *Obviously, the more participation one has had in other social groups outside of work, the easier it is to set up alternative activities and support. With the workplace demanding so much of people's lives, having a broader range of social participation and support can be especially difficult. This is where community meeting places and coffee houses, places where you can drop in and talk or play a game, become lifesaving.'*

PLAN TO EXPERIENCE

It's important to set goals but it's more important to take action. All too often people set goals without really working out whether what they're aiming for is what they truly want. Rather than feeling bad because you didn't meet your list of goals, you can choose to feel excited because you will first try out different things. If you're not sure what job you want, where you want to live, what kind of relationship you want, if you have no idea what life you really want except that you don't like yours, then you can turn this into an adventure.

KELE BAKER ON RAW EXPERIENCES

- *'Analysis leads to paralysis: if all you do is think about what you don't want or might want, you risk staying stuck.*
- *When you don't know what you want, a good thing to do is dabble and explore.*
- *Have a raw experience with no expectation. Go to a new area, pub, class, workshop, gym, anything. From each raw experience you learn. "I liked ... but I didn't feel comfortable about ... I enjoyed ... but I know next time I will ..."*

> • *Putting yourself in different environments triggers new awareness – and potentially new desires. Staying in the same environment with the same routine doesn't allow for a new desire to be awakened.'*

HOLIDAYS: PAUSE AND PONDER, REFLECT AND RESET

It's easy to let life slip by so that daily routine takes over and you're either chasing your tail unable to find time to make changes to get out of a rut, or you feel you're wading through mud. One way to handle this is to go with how the year is structured: there is Christmas, New Year, Easter and public holidays. You can use these times to pause and ponder on where you're at, reflect on what you need to do, and reset your mind to taking new actions. If you're able to go on holiday, then this gives you extra time to reflect.

As we go from autumn to winter and nature hibernates, this is a natural time for reflection. In the spring, by Easter when the days are sunnier and longer, we naturally feel an impulse to do more. You have the energy of nature to help you plan. Let's be honest, if you loathe exercise and make a resolution in January when it's wet and cold to go running, are you going to do it? No.

Preparation sets you up for action. Actions make you feel good. Think about what you instinctively do when you book a bargain air flight and are taking your luggage on board. You check the measurements and weight allowed, and then you figure out how you're going to manage this requirement with what you need for your trip. So you get creative about finding solutions, you even get excited about that mac with huge pockets, that case that's super light, and you buy your toiletries at the airport. You find creative ways to handle the luggage problem and the time spent doing so pays off. It's the same in life. Taking some time out to reflect and plan not only is part of reenergizing your mind (so that it can build that willpower muscle too), this time to reflect catapults you forward.

> ❝You can dream big or small. Dream big and then plan the small details. Or see how you can grow the smallest idea.❞

Dannie-Lu Carr, creativity specialist, communications consultant & creative practitioner

Now you have what you need to stay on track every day so that you don't lose sight of your inner and outer ambitions. As we said in Chapter 3, real ambition is a match – a match between inner and outer expressions of you. Changing your morning routine so it's not frenetic, setting yourself up to have a good day every day and achieving one thing – something (however small) every day, being prepared to handle difficult people and making a conscious effort to *be* with actual not virtual people in a meaningful way, and giving yourself time to recharge and reflect will, we hope, become a welcome routine. This routine or way of life will feed your desires – your ambitions – so that they become a reality. And that reality is your success.

ASK YOURSELF

(Q) I can improve my morning routine by ...

(Q) One thing I can change to make my day better is ...

(Q) The person I most need to plan how to handle is ...

(Q) To rest properly I can ...

(Q) The pop song that always makes me feel fantastic when I sing the words is ...

(Q) Why don't I just have a go at ...?

(Q) The next holiday coming up is .... so I'm going to use the time to ...

WHAT NEXT?

We hope that you are feeling inspired to investigate your dreams, and that above all you feel confident that it's possible to make them happen. We're not claiming that you will achieve success only by doing x, y, z because there are no magic formulas. Our philosophy is based on enjoying the process of discovering what makes you happy and feels right for you. It's natural for everyone to want something different, something better, something more – this is what makes us human beings. Ambition comes in many forms, and so definitions of success will vary. What's important is that you find your unique definition of success, based on the way you want to live your life. Then your ambition to make this happen will have the right impetus.

What next? You will be looking within to match your personality, strengths and talents with your dreams. Life isn't just about work, so these dreams will include all aspects of life. Then you can proceed with the process in between of making it all happen. That's healthy ambition.

We've provided you with the tools to be your own analyst and coach. Through our coaching questions and tests you can discover what you have and what you want. With the latest scientific research that we've given you, you'll be able to make informed evaluations of where you're at, and with our expert panel's advice you have the top-level guidance for the journey to your success.

Perhaps you have got to this point having read the book slowly, answering the questions and completing the tests; or you may have read everything with the intention of going back to complete the questions and tests. You may even have read random chapters with the titles that resonated first. We don't insist there is a right way of going about it. Starting with this book, you can choose your own process of mastering what you need to learn to achieve your fulfilled life.

The one thing we do believe is that ambition isn't something that can be picked up whenever someone decides they have more time. Creating your successful life means living the desire to do so on a daily basis. However you choose to do this is up to you, and we hope this book has given you plenty of advice so that you can confidently fuel your desires every day. Healthy ambition is about creating a fulfilled life, and a *full* life needs *filling* every day that we live.

You may have started reading this book thinking that ambition is about making a career happen, or that success = money. We've given you a new way to consider ambition and success. Healthy ambition isn't one dimensional – it's not just about the job or just about marriage or just about anything. So the next step is for you to create your blueprint of success and of course to take the practical steps of making your dreams in all dimensions of your life happen.

We wish you an exciting journey. Do let us know what your travels are like and where you arrive. We wish you all the best.

ABOUT PSYCHOLOGIES

MAGAZINE

Psychologies is a magazine read by those who want to lead a fulfilling life, who want to live a life on their own terms, however you choose to define it. *Psychologies* helps you discover what 'life success' looks like for you – from the inside out.

We're on a mission to find out from the best experts and latest research in psychology how we can all lead happier and more fulfilling lives. *Psychologies* is not about striving to do more but rather finding ways to BE more. Who are you? And what do you really want? These are questions we're always asking ourselves. *Psychologies* magazine is about being the best you, and we mean being in an active way: becoming the best you can be, the happiest and the most fulfilled you.

We focus on helping you understand yourself and the world around you, by gathering the latest, most compelling thinking and translating it into practical wisdom that can support you as you create the life that works for you.

Real Ambition is written by Lorna V, who also wrote the first book in our series, *Real Confidence*. Lorna graduated from the London School of Economics and then followed her dream to be a journalist working for national newspapers and magazines. She has a specific interest in ambition and success as for over a decade she has also been lecturing in journalism and running writing workshops. To help new writers find their authentic voice and achieve success she draws as much on her interest in psychology as her wide-ranging experience as a journalist. She has been shortlisted for the Verity Bargate theatre award and recently embarked on performing her own work as an actor.

www.LornaV.com @LornaVwriter

REFERENCES

CHAPTER 1

1. NIH/National Institute of Mental Health. 2015. 'Our brain's secrets to success? Unique support system promotes cortex growth, connectivity linked to prowess.' *ScienceDaily*, 29 September 2015: www.sciencedaily.com/releases/2015/09/150929092851.htm.
2. www.greenschool.org/.
3. *TIME Magazine*, Inc. 2005. Cover Story, November 14, 2005. (pp. 48–59).
4. www.psychologies.co.uk/work/is-ambition-a-dirty-word.html.

CHAPTER 2

1. Society for Personality and Social Psychology. 2015. 'Can money buy happiness? The relationship between money and well-being.' *ScienceDaily*, 28 February 2015: www.sciencedaily.com/releases/2015/02/150228084708.htm.
2. Cameron Anderson, Michael W. Kraus, Dacher Keltner et al. 2012. 'The local-ladder effect: social status and subjective well-being.' *Psychological Science*. DOI: 10.1177/0956797611434537; Association for Psychological Science. 2012. 'Respect matters more than money for happiness in life.' *ScienceDaily*, 20 June 2012: www.sciencedaily.com/releases/2012/06/120620133310.htm.
3. American Psychological Association. 2011. 'Money can't buy happiness: Individualism a stronger predictor of well-being than wealth, says new study.' *ScienceDaily*, 14 June 2011: www.sciencedaily.com/releases/2011/06/110614100521.htm.
4. Christian Bayer and Falko Jüssen. 2015. 'Happiness and the persistence of income shocks.' *American Economic Journal: Macroeconomics* 7(4): 160. DOI: 10.1257/mac.20120163

5. Universität Bonn. 2015; 'New formula for life-satisfaction.' *ScienceDaily*, 1 October 2015: www.sciencedaily.com/releases/2015/10/151001095411.htm.

6. Vanderbilt University. 2014. 'Gifted men and women define success differently, 40-year study finds.' *ScienceDaily*, 19 November 2014: www.sciencedaily.com/releases/2014/11/141119101700.htm.

7. Sustainable Development Solutions Network. 2015. 'World Happiness Report 2015 ranks happiest countries.' *ScienceDaily*, 23 April 2015: www.sciencedaily.com/releases/2015/04/150423130327.htm.

8. University of Rochester. 2009. 'Achieving fame, wealth and beauty are psychological dead ends, study says.' *ScienceDaily*, 19 May 2009: www.sciencedaily.com/releases/2009/05/090514111402.htm.

9. University of Colorado at Boulder. 2014. 'Experiences make people happier than material goods, says University of Colorado prof.' *ScienceDaily*, 28 December 2004: www.sciencedaily.com/releases/2004/12/041219182811.htm.

10. Daniel H. Pink. 2010. *Drive: The Surprising Truth About What Motivates Us*, Canongate.

11. Edward Deci. 1971. 'Effects of external rewards on motivation', *Journal of Social Psychology* 18: 105–115.

12. *TIME Magazine*, Inc. 2005. Cover Story November 14, 2005 (pp. 48–59).

13. Duncan Coppock. 2005. *The Self Factor: The Power of Being You: A Coaching Approach*, Findhorn.

CHAPTER 3

1. John Purkiss and David Royston-Lee. 2009. Brand You: Turn your Unique Talents into a Winning Formula, Pearson.

2. Ibid.

3. www.milliemarotta.co.uk.

4. www.theworlds50best.com/list/1-50-winners/El-Celler-de-Can-Roca; www.tripadvisor.co.uk/Restaurant_Review-g187499-d996088-Reviews-El_Celler_de_Can_Roca-Girona_Province_of_Girona_Catalonia.html.

5. www.cookingonabootstrap.com.
6. Mihaly Csikszentmihalyi. 2000. *Beyond Boredom and Anxiety: Experiencing Flow in Work and Play*, Wiley.
7. www. heymarci.com.
8. www.ellemacpherson.com.
9. www.welleco.co.uk.
10. www.dailymail.co.uk/femail/article-2690780/Why-Britains-models-SIXTY-As-retailers-chase-grey-pound-never-older-women-topping-pensions-2-000-modelling-jobs.html.

CHAPTER 4

1. University of Essex, Social and Economic Research. 'Big sisters do better: New study of siblings finds eldest girls have the edge.' *ScienceDaily*, 2 May 2014. www.sciencedaily.com/releases/2014/05/140502160429.htm.
2. American Friends of Tel Aviv University. 2012. 'Intelligence is more accurate predictor of future career success than socioeconomic background, study suggests.' *ScienceDaily*, 29 March 2012: www.sciencedaily.com/releases/2012/03/120329142035.htm.
3. Daniel H. Pink. 2010. *Drive: The Surprising Truth About What Motivates Us*, Canongate.
4. Richard M. Ryan and Edward L. Deci. 2000. 'Self determination theory and the facilitation of intrinsic motivation, social development, and well-being.' *American Psychologist* 55: 68–78.
5. Carol S. Dweck, 1999. *Self Theories: Their Role in Motivation, Personality and Development*, Psychology Press.
6. www.mindsetonline.com.
7. www. graphics8.nytimes.com/images/blogs/freakonomics/pdf/DeliberatePractice (PsychologicalReview.pdf).
8. www.imdb.com/name/nm0000093/bio.
9. www.sites.sas.upenn.edu/duckworth.
10. Angela L. Duckworth, Christopher Peterson, Michael D. Matthews and Dennis R Kelly. 2007. 'Grit: perseverance and passion for long term goals.' *Journal of Personality and Social Psychology* 92: 1087–1111.
11. Angela Duckworth, P. Quinn and M. Seligman. 2009. 'Positive predictors of teacher effectiveness.' *Journal of Positive Psychology* 19: 540–547.

CHAPTER 5

1. Association for Psychological Science. 2011. 'Standing tall is key for success: "Powerful postures" may trump title and rank.' *ScienceDaily*. 7 January 2011: www.sciencedaily.com/releases/2011/01/110106145257.htm

2. https://www.ted.com/speakers/amy_cuddy.

3. William E. Copeland, Dieter Wolke, Lilly Shanahan, and E Jane Costello. 2015. 'Adult functional outcomes of common childhood psychiatric problems: a prospective, longitudinal study.' *JAMA Psychiatry*. DOI: 10.1001/jamapsychiatry.2015.0730; Duke Medicine. 'Success in adulthood linked to childhood psychiatric health.' *ScienceDaily*, 15 July 2015: www.sciencedaily.com/releases/2015/07/150715113655.htm.

4. Galena K. Rhoades and Lisa F. Wood. 2014. 'Family conflict and college-student social adjustment: the mediating role of emotional distress about the family.' *Couple and Family Psychology: Research and Practice* 3(3): 156–164. DOI: http://dx.doi.org/10.1037/cfp0000024.

CHAPTER 6

1. Public Library of Science. 2012. 'Working too much is correlated with two-fold increase in likelihood of depression.' *ScienceDaily*. 26 January 2012: www.sciencedaily.com/releases/2012/01/120125172317.htm.

2. Cell Press. 2009. 'Brain mechanisms of social conformity.' *ScienceDaily*. 16 January 2009: www.sciencedaily.com/releases/2009/01/090114124109.htm.

3. York University. 2014. 'Perfectionism can lead to imperfect health: high achievers more prone to emotional, physical and relationship problems.' *ScienceDaily*. 14 June 2004: www.sciencedaily.com/releases/2004/06/040614074620.htm.

4. www.goodreads.com/author/show/904939.Terry_Hayes.

5. www.gillian-flynn.com/about-gillian/.

6. www.theguardian.com/books/2015/apr/21/the-girl-on-the-train-paula-hawkins-new-gone-girl-female-thriller-authors-gillian-flynn.

7. www.americanexpress.com/us/small-business/openforum/ articles/13-business-leaders-who-failed-before-they-succeeded.
8. University of California, Berkeley. 2014. 'Wealth, power or lack thereof at heart of many mental disorders.' *ScienceDaily*, 9 December 2014: www.sciencedaily.com/ releases/2014/12/141209082351.htm.

CHAPTER 7

1. Roy F. Baumeister and John Tierney. 2012. *Willpower: Rediscovering Our Greatest Strength*, Penguin.
2. Ibid.
3. Ibid., p. 36.
4. *Journal of Consumer Research*, Inc. 2015. 'Trying to project an image of success? It could make you dwell on your failures.' *ScienceDaily*, 22 January 2015: www.sciencedaily.com/ releases/2015/01/150122084342.htm.
5. *Psychologies Magazine* February 2012 issue.
6. Roy F. Baumeister and John Tierney. 2012. *Willpower: Rediscovering Our Greatest Strength*, Penguin, p. 44.
7. Ibid., p. 49
8. Kelly McGonigal. 2012. *Maximum Willpower*, Macmillan.
9. www.online.stanford.edu/course/science-willpower-and-change.
10. *Psychologies Magazine* February 2012 issue.
11. www.heidigranthalvorson.com.
12. Heidi Grant Halvorson. 2010. *Succeed, How we Reach our Goals*, Plume Penguin, pp. 14–20.
13. H. Grant and C. S. Dweck. 2003. 'Clarifying achievement goals and their impact.' *Journal of Personality and Social Psychology* 85(3): 541–553.
14. Heidi Grant Halvorson. 2010. *Succeed, How we Reach our Goals*, Plume Penguin, p. 66.

CHAPTER 8

1. Ohio State University. 2014. 'In a bad mood? Head to Facebook and find someone worse off.' *ScienceDaily*, 2 October 2014: www .sciencedaily.com/releases/2014/10/141002123058.htm.

2. Heather Mendick, Kim Allen and Laura Harvey. 2015. '"We can get everything we want if we try hard": young people, celebrity, hard work.' *British Journal of Educational Studies* 1. DOI:10. 1080/00071005.2014.1002382; www.sciencedaily.com/releases/2015/02/150227084557.htm.

3. www.dailystar.co.uk/showbiz/481647/X-Factor-scandal-Louisa-Johnson-pro-singing-lessons.

4. www.alexandraburkeofficial.com/home.

5. www.fastcompany.com/59549/failure-doesnt-suck.

6. www.yanisvaroufakis.eu/about/.

7. www.behindthehustle.com/2011/09/michael-jordan-succeeded-because-he-failed/.

8. University of Exeter. 2008. 'How stereotypes can lead to success, psychologists explain.' *ScienceDaily*, 22 April 2008: www.sciencedaily.com/releases/2008/04/080421191418.htm.

9. www.carl-jung.net/collective_unconscious.html.

10. www.bsu.edu/classes/magrath/205resources/pearson/pearson.html; www.carolspearson.com/about/.

11. *Brand You: Turn Your Unique Talents into a Winning Formula*, John Purkiss and David Royston-Lee, Pearson Education Limited. ©, John Purkiss and David Royston-Lee (2012).

12. Ibid.

13. Ibid.

CHAPTER 9

1. Roy F. Baumeister and John Tierney. 2012. *Willpower: Rediscovering Our Greatest Strength*, Penguin, p. 66.

2. 'Conflict among personal strivings: Immediate and long-term implications for psychological and physical well-being'. www.psycnet.apa.org/index.cfm?fa=buy.optionToBuy&id=1988-32654-001.

3. 'Unleash your willpower.' *Psychologies Magazine* March 2012.

4. www.dash.harvard.edu/bitstream/handle/1/3685822/Christakis_DynamicSpreadHappinessSupplement.pdf?sequence=3.

5. Gabriele Oettingen. 2014. *Rethinking Positive Thinking – Inside the New Science of Motivation*, Penguin.

6.   Peter M. Gollwitzer. 1999. 'Implementation intentions: Strong effects of simple plans.' *American Psychologist* 54: 493–503.

CHAPTER 10

1.   www.sciencedaily.com/releases/2012/03/120314170647.htm.
2.   L. Fortlouis Wood. 2012. 'Leadership, trust, and cooperation: Implications for community building in multicultural settings', in P. Cunningham and N. Fretwell (eds) *Creating Communities: Local, National and Global*. CiCe, pp. 366–377.

Notes

Notes

Notes